Edward FitzGerald's
Rubáiyát of Omar Khayyám

T0275316

Edward FitzGerald's *Rubáiyát of Omar Khayyám*

A Famous Poem and Its Influence

Edited by
William H. Martin and Sandra Mason

ANTHEM PRESS
LONDON · NEW YORK · DELHI

Anthem Press
An imprint of Wimbledon Publishing Company
www.anthempress.com

This edition first published in UK and USA 2011
by ANTHEM PRESS
75-76 Blackfriars Road, London SE1 8HA, UK
or PO Box 9779, London SW19 7ZG, UK
and
244 Madison Ave. #116, New York, NY 10016, USA

Cover image: illustration by Doris M. Palmer for quatrain 27
in the first edition of the *Rubáiyát*, published by Leopold B. Hill, London, 1921.

British Library Cataloguing in Publication Data
A catalogue record for this book is available from the British Library.

Library of Congress Cataloging-in-Publication Data
Edward FitzGerald's Rubáiyát of Omar Khayyám : a famous poem and its
influence / edited by William H. Martin and Sandra Mason.
p. cm.
Includes bibliographical references and index.
ISBN-13: 978-0-85728-770-0 (pbk. : alk. paper)
ISBN-10: 0-85728-770-2 (pbk. : alk. paper)
1. Omar Khayyam. Ruba'iyat. 2. FitzGerald, Edward, 1809–1883–Criticism and
interpretation. I. Martin, W. H. (William Henry), 1927- II. Mason, Sandra.
PK6525.E36 2011
891'.5511–dc22
2011014787

ISBN-13: 978 0 85728 770 0 (Pbk)
ISBN-10: 0 85728 770 2 (Pbk)

This title is also available as an eBook.

Contents

Figure 1 Edward FitzGerald – the philosopher pose.

Introduction

The *Rubáiyát of Omar Khayyám* is one of the best known poems in the world. It has been continuously in publication for well over a century and there have been translations into more than 85 different languages. Yet there are many young people, and some older ones, who have never heard the verses, and know nothing of their fascinating content and history. The poem has been neglected in the recent study of English literature, despite the fact that it is the English version, created by the Victorian writer Edward FitzGerald, that brought this work of Persian origins to worldwide fame.

What is the reason for this paradoxical situation? Much has been said and written on this subject, especially in 2009 during the celebrations of 150 years since the first publication of FitzGerald's *Rubáiyát* and 200 years since the poet's birth. It is not our intention to review these questions in detail here. Our aims are different and they are three-fold:

- to present the poem to new readers, especially those of the younger generation, in an authentic but accessible way;
- to tell the story of the poem's origins and subsequent history, based on the latest available research;
- to discuss the continuing relevance of the verses and their message in the new world of the twenty-first century.

Behind these aims lies our belief that the *Rubáiyát* is an important poem which deserves serious attention. FitzGerald's verses, his imagery and use of the English language have made an enduring contribution to English literature, art and music. Their influence can be found in many aspects of our culture, right up to the present day. In terms of content also, it is evident from the 2009 celebrations, and the schools' projects that were part of them, that the *Rubáiyát* still speaks to people of all ages. The poem deals with eternal questions about life, such as 'where do we come from?', 'why are we here?' and 'where are we going?', and it has an ambivalence of view on these issues that is part of its attraction.

In terms of layout, our book is designed first and foremost to let FitzGerald's *Rubáiyát* speak for itself. We have therefore put the text of the *Rubáiyát* right at the beginning; it comes in Part 1 immediately after this short introduction. Despite being over 150 years old, the verses are still approachable and easy to read; their colourful language, the images and the simple rhyming pattern all make them very memorable and worth reading without further explanation, though understanding the full meaning of the words is helped by more analysis and background.

Readers who prefer to know more about the poem before reading it may wish to start with Part 2 of the book. This provides a commentary on the background to the *Rubáiyát*, its meaning and its influence. Part 2 deals successively with the origins of the *Rubáiyát of Omar Khayyám* (page 93), how Edward FitzGerald came to create the English poem (page 97), the form and structure of the poem (page 105), how it became popular (page 111), the history of its emergence into worldwide fame (page 117), the exploitation of the poem in various ways (page 121) and the relevance of the poem to the changing world over 150 years (page 129). Our comments complement FitzGerald's own Notes and Prefaces, which come in Part 1, immediately after the text of the poem (page 65).

Further notes and references, including a glossary of key words, are in Part 3 (page 143). For the new reader, a couple of early explanations may be useful. A *rubáiyát* is a collection of four line verses; one such verse is called a *rubái*, and quatrain is the equivalent English name. The Omar Khayyám, who is the apparent author of the *rubáiyát* that were the basis for FitzGerald's poem, was an astronomer and mathematician living in Persia (Iran) in the eleventh and twelfth centuries. But, as we see in Part 2 (page 94), there is a mystery about whether the historical Khayyám actually composed the verses that are attributed to him.

Acknowledgements

In preparing this edition of the *Rubáiyát of Omar Khayyám,* we have drawn on a long tradition of scholarship in many fields. This ranges from research on mediaeval Persia and its poetry to modern work on English literature, and from the study of book illustration to the social analysis of advertising and brand promotion. The scholars on whose work we have drawn specifically are named in the notes and references.

We acknowledge particularly the work of other recent editors of editions of the *Rubáiyát,* notably (in order of date of publication) Dick Davis, Christopher Decker, Daniel Karlin and Anthony Briggs. We are also grateful for the many insights gained from our interaction with other specialists and collectors, especially Garry Garrard, and our two colleagues from the Netherlands, Jos Biegstraaten and Jos Coumans.

Above all, we should like to pay tribute to the stimulus we received from the many people and organisations who worked so hard to create the celebratory events in the Year of the Rubaiyat in 2009. They are listed in detail on our website, www.omarkhayyamrubaiyat.com/2009events. They provided us with the opportunity to develop our own ideas about the *Rubáiyát* and to exchange them with other enthusiasts. The creative reactions of the young people in Cambridgeshire and elsewhere to this famous poem were a particular pleasure and encouragement. So too has been our co-operation with Adrian Poole and Christine van Ruymbeke, and individual authors, in the editing of the volume of essays resulting from the 2009 FitzGerald conference in Cambridge.

Our thanks are also due to Anthem Press, both for commissioning this new edition of the *Rubáiyát* and for the help of their staff and three anonymous reviewers in bringing the project to completion. Among others whom we must thank are the following: Michael Langford, for help in locating and translating FitzGerald's references to the Greek version of Aristophanes' *The Wasps*; Jos Coumans, for providing us with the artwork for Figure 7; and Suzanne Jones, for permission to reproduce her painting as Figure 9. We have attempted where relevant to locate copyright holders for other illustrations used in the book, and we should be glad to hear from any that we have failed to find.

List of Illustrations

Part 1

Edward FitzGerald's
Rubáiyát of Omar Khayyám

A Note on the Texts

In this part of the book, we present the text of Edward FitzGerald's *Rubáiyát of Omar Khayyám*, together with his Notes and Prefaces to the poem. The nature of FitzGerald's *Rubáiyát* and its history are discussed in more detail in Part 2 (especially page 105). A few points of clarification here may be helpful to the new reader. First, FitzGerald did not make a direct or literal translation from Omar Khayyám's Persian verses. This is why we talk of him 'creating' his *Rubáiyát*. His aim was to interpret the thinking of the original and to 'render' it (his words) into good English verse. He did, however, retain the four-line verse structure and rhyming scheme from the Persian. Second, FitzGerald departed from the original Persian in giving his poem an overall story line. The *Rubáiyát* tells of a day in the life of the poet, voicing his thoughts and concerns. There is also an important section towards the end which is set in the potter's shop; this is called the *Kúza-Náma* (Book of the Pots) in the first edition (see Part 2, page 108 for more on the poem's structure and themes).

Anyone skipping quickly forward will see that we have actually included three texts of FitzGerald's poem. Edward FitzGerald produced four different versions of his *Rubáiyát* in his lifetime, the first published in 1859, and subsequent ones in 1868, 1872, 1879; a fifth edition was published posthumously in 1889. In creating successive versions of his *Rubáiyát*, FitzGerald was responding to new Persian sources and demands from his publisher, as well as his own changes in interpretation. FitzGerald altered the wording of some verses between the different editions and added and deleted verses in his successive versions; the total number of verses goes from 75 in the first edition to 110 in the second and 101 in the final three editions.*

---

* To help the reader, we have marked the addition and deletion of verses on the texts:

   # indicates a new verse in the edition.

   Ø indicates a verse deleted in subsequent editions.

We have shown here the texts of FitzGerald's first, second and fourth editions. The fourth edition has been chosen since it is the final one that FitzGerald himself approved for publication; the third and fifth versions are virtually identical to the fourth, with only minor differences in punctuation. The three texts shown give readers access to the main versions of FitzGerald's *Rubáiyát* and allow them to see for themselves the poet's evolving solutions to an eternal problem: how to express the thoughts in one's mind in a form that satisfies the writer, and is attractive to the reader. The changes that FitzGerald made over time to the structure and detail of his poem provide an important insight into the creative process. There is a table in Part 3 (page 148) which relates the numbering of the equivalent verses (quatrains), from the same Persian original, in different editions, making it easier to compare the changes in wording.

The question of the 'best' version of the *Rubáiyát* has been much debated; did FitzGerald improve on his first version, were his revisions and second thoughts generally a mistake, or is this a subject on which no judgement is possible? Views on this vary greatly and editors over the years have adopted different ways of presenting the poem; contrast, for example, the new editions by Karlin and Briggs in 2009 referenced on page 161. As editors, we believe that readers should have the chance to make their own judgement and establish their own preferences between the editions. Our personal favourite is undoubtedly the first edition, though we acknowledge that some of the additional quatrains included in the second edition are also memorable.

Immediately following the three texts of the *Rubáiyát*, we have put versions of FitzGerald's own Notes, which clarify various points in individual verses,[†] and of his explanatory Prefaces to the poem. Our texts are both 'composite' versions, in that they combine material from all the editions of the *Rubáiyát*. In fact, FitzGerald made mostly minor changes to his Notes and Prefaces between the editions and our versions are based mainly on the fourth edition of the *Rubáiyát* with some additions from earlier versions. More information on the texts used and other editorial notes are given in Part 3 (page 143). This includes comments on FitzGerald's idiosyncratic spelling and punctuation, which we have retained as far as possible, and details of the key books that he referenced in his Notes and Prefaces.

[†] Numbers in brackets [1] refer to FitzGerald's Notes, which start on page 65.

First Edition (1859)

1

AWAKE! for Morning in the Bowl of Night
Has flung the Stone that puts the Stars to Flight:[1]
   And Lo! the Hunter of the East has caught
The Sultán's Turret in a Noose of Light.

2

Dreaming when Dawn's Left Hand was in the Sky[2]
I heard a Voice within the Tavern cry,
   "Awake, my Little ones, and fill the Cup
"Before Life's Liquor in its Cup be dry."

3

And, as the Cock crew, those who stood before
The Tavern shouted—"Open then the Door!
   "You know how little while we have to stay,
"And, once departed, may return no more."

4

Now the New Year[3] reviving old Desires,
The thoughtful Soul to Solitude retires,
   Where the WHITE HAND OF MOSES on the Bough
Puts out,[4] and Jesus from the Ground suspires.

5

Irám indeed is gone with all its Rose,[5]
And Jamshýd's Sev'n-ring'd Cup where no one knows;
   But still the Vine her ancient Ruby yields,
And still a Garden by the Water blows.

6

And David's Lips are lock't; but in divine
High piping Péhlevi,[6] with "Wine! Wine! Wine!
   "*Red* Wine!"—the Nightingale cries to the Rose
That yellow Cheek[7] of her's to'incarnadine.

7

Come, fill the Cup, and in the Fire of Spring
The Winter Garment of Repentance fling:
   The Bird of Time has but a little way
To fly—and Lo! the Bird is on the Wing.

8

And look—a thousand Blossoms with the Day
Woke—and a thousand scatter'd into Clay:
   And this first Summer Month that brings the Rose
Shall take Jamshýd and Kaikobád away.

9

But come with old Khayyám, and leave the Lot
Of Kaikobád and Kaikhosrú forgot:
   Let Rustum lay about him as he will,[8]
Or Hátim Tai cry Supper—heed them not.

10

With me along some Strip of Herbage strown
That just divides the desert from the sown,
   Where name of Slave and Sultán scarce is known,
And pity Sultán Máhmúd on his Throne.

11

Here with a Loaf of Bread beneath the Bough,
A Flask of Wine, a Book of Verse—and Thou
　　Beside me singing in the Wilderness—
And Wilderness is Paradise enow.

12

"How sweet is mortal Sovranty!"—think some:
Others—"How blest the Paradise to come!"
　　Ah, take the Cash in hand and waive the Rest;
Oh, the brave Music of a *distant* Drum![9]

13

Look to the Rose that blows about us—"Lo,
"Laughing," she says, "into the World I blow:
　　"At once the silken Tassel of my Purse
"Tear, and its Treasure[10] on the Garden throw."

14

The Worldly Hope men set their Hearts upon
Turns Ashes—or it prospers; and anon,
　　Like Snow upon the Desert's dusty Face
Lighting a little Hour or two—is gone.

15

And those who husbanded the Golden Grain,
And those who flung it to the Winds like Rain,
　　Alike to no such aureate Earth are turn'd
As, buried once, Men want dug up again.

16

Think, in this batter'd Caravanserai
Whose Doorways are alternate Night and Day,
    How Sultán after Sultán with his Pomp
Abode his Hour or two, and went his way.

17

They say the Lion and the Lizard keep
The Courts where Jamshýd gloried and drank deep:[11] [13]
    And Bahrám, that great Hunter—the Wild Ass[12]
Stamps o'er his Head, and he lies fast asleep.

18

I sometimes think that never blows so red
The Rose as where some buried Caesar bled;
    That every Hyacinth the Garden wears
Dropt in its Lap from some once lovely Head.

19

And this delightful Herb whose tender Green
Fledges the River's Lip on which we lean—
    Ah, lean upon it lightly! for who knows
From what once lovely Lip it springs unseen!

20

Ah, my Belovéd, fill the Cup that clears
To-day of past Regrets and future Fears—
    To-morrow?—Why, To-morrow I may be
Myself with Yesterday's Sev'n Thousand Years.[15]

21

Lo! some we loved, the loveliest and best
That Time and Fate of all their Vintage prest,
    Have drunk their Cup a Round or two before,
And one by one crept silently to Rest.

22

And we, that now make merry in the Room
They left, and Summer dresses in new Bloom,
    Ourselves must we beneath the Couch of Earth
Descend, ourselves to make a Couch—for whom?

23

Ah, make the most of what we yet may spend,
Before we too into the Dust descend;
    Dust into Dust, and under Dust, to lie,
Sans Wine, sans Song, sans Singer, and—sans End!

24

Alike for those who for To-DAY prepare,
And those that after a To-MORROW stare,
    A Muezzín from the Tower of Darkness cries
"Fools! your Reward is neither Here nor There!"

25

Why, all the Saints and Sages who discuss'd
Of the Two Worlds so learnedly, are thrust
    Like foolish Prophets forth; their Words to Scorn
Are scatter'd, and their Mouths are stopt with Dust.

26

Oh, come with old Khayyám, and leave the Wise
To talk; one thing is certain, that Life flies;
　　One thing is certain, and the Rest is Lies;
The Flower that once has blown for ever dies.

27

Myself when young did eagerly frequent
Doctor and Saint, and heard great Argument
　　About it and about: but evermore
Came out by the same Door as in I went.

28

With them the Seed of Wisdom did I sow,
And with my own hand labour'd it to grow:
　　And this was all the Harvest that I reap'd—
"I came like Water, and like Wind I go."

29

Into this Universe, and *why* not knowing,
Nor *whence*, like Water willy-nilly flowing:
　　And out of it, as Wind along the Waste,
I know not *whither*, willy-nilly blowing.

30

What, without asking, hither hurried *whence?*
And, without asking, *whither* hurried hence!
　　Another and another Cup to drown
The Memory of this Impertinence!

31

Up from Earth's Centre through the Seventh Gate
I rose, and on the Throne of Saturn sate,[16]
    And many Knots unravel'd by the Road;
But not the Knot of Human Death and Fate.

32

There was a Door to which I found no Key:
There was a Veil past which I could not see:
    Some little Talk awhile of ME and THEE
There seemed—and then no more of THEE and ME.[17]

33

Then to the rolling Heav'n itself I cried,
Asking, "What Lamp had Destiny to guide
    "Her little Children stumbling in the Dark?"
And—"A blind Understanding!" Heav'n replied.

34

Then to this earthen Bowl did I adjourn
My Lip the secret Well of Life to learn:
    And Lip to Lip it murmur'd—"While you live
"Drink!—for once dead you never shall return."

35

I think the Vessel, that with fugitive
Articulation answer'd, once did live,
    And merry-make; and the cold Lip I kiss'd
How many Kisses might it take—and give!

36

For in the Market-place, one Dusk of Day,
I watch'd the Potter thumping his wet Clay:
   And with its all obliterated Tongue
It murmur'd—"Gently, Brother, gently, pray!"

37 Ø

Ah, fill the Cup:—what boots it to repeat
How Time is slipping underneath our Feet:
   Unborn TO-MORROW, and dead YESTERDAY,
Why fret about them if TO-DAY be sweet!

38

One Moment in Annihilation's Waste,
One Moment, of the Well of Life to taste—
   The Stars are setting and the Caravan
Starts for the Dawn of Nothing[21]—Oh, make haste!

39

How long, how long, in infinite Pursuit
Of This and That endeavour and dispute?
   Better be merry with the fruitful Grape
Than sadden after none, or bitter, Fruit.

40

You know, my Friends, how long since in my House
For a new Marriage I did make Carouse:
   Divorced old barren Reason from my Bed,
And took the Daughter of the Vine to Spouse.

41

For "Is" and "Is-NOT" though *with* Rule and Line,
And "UP-AND-DOWN" *without*, I could define,[23]
   I yet in all I only cared to know,
Was never deep in anything but—Wine.

42

And lately, by the Tavern Door agape,
Came stealing through the Dusk an Angel Shape
   Bearing a Vessel on his Shoulder; and
He bid me taste of it; and 'twas—the Grape!

43

The Grape that can with Logic absolute
The Two-and-Seventy jarring Sects[24] confute:
   The subtle Alchemist that in a Trice
Life's leaden Metal into Gold transmute.

44

The mighty Mahmúd, the victorious Lord,
That all the misbelieving and black Horde[25]
   Of Fears and Sorrows that infest the Soul
Scatters and slays with his enchanted Sword.

45 Ø

But leave the Wise to wrangle, and with me
The Quarrel of the Universe let be:
   And, in some corner of the Hubbub coucht,
Make Game of that which makes as much of Thee.

46

For in and out, above, about, below,
'Tis nothing but a Magic Shadow-show,
   Play'd in a Box whose Candle is the Sun,
Round which we Phantom Figures come and go.[26]

47

And if the Wine you drink, the Lip you press,
End in the Nothing all Things end in—Yes—
   Then fancy while Thou art, Thou art but what
Thou shalt be—Nothing—Thou shalt not be less.

48

While the Rose blows along the River Brink,
With old Khayyám the Ruby Vintage drink:
   And when the Angel with his darker Draught
Draws up to Thee—take that, and do not shrink.

49

'Tis all a Chequer-board of Nights and Days
Where Destiny with Men for Pieces plays:
   Hither and thither moves, and mates, and slays,
And one by one back in the Closet lays.

50

The Ball no Question makes of Ayes and Noes,
But Right or Left as strikes the Player goes;
   And He that toss'd Thee down into the Field,
He knows about it all—HE knows—HE knows![27]

51

The Moving Finger writes; and, having writ,
Moves on: nor all thy Piety nor Wit
   Shall lure it back to cancel half a Line,
Nor all thy Tears wash out a Word of it.

52

And that inverted Bowl we call The Sky,
Whereunder crawling coop't we live and die,
   Lift not thy hands to *It* for help—for It
Rolls impotently on as Thou or I.

53

With Earth's first Clay They did the Last Man's knead,
And then of the Last Harvest sow'd the Seed:
   Yea, the first Morning of Creation wrote
What the Last Dawn of Reckoning shall read.

54

I tell Thee this—When, starting from the Goal,
Over the shoulders of the flaming Foal
   Of Heav'n Parwín and Mushtara they flung,[28]
In my predestin'd Plot of Dust and Soul

55

The Vine had struck a Fibre; which about
If clings my Being—let the Súfi flout;
   Of my Base Metal may be filed a Key,
That shall unlock the Door he howls without.

56

And this I know: whether the one True Light,
Kindle to Love, or Wrathconsume me quite,
    One Glimpse of It within the Tavern caught
Better than in the Temple lost outright.

57

Oh Thou, who didst with Pitfall and with Gin
Beset the Road I was to wander in,
    Thou wilt not with Predestination round
Enmesh me, and impute my Fall to Sin?

58

Oh, Thou, who Man of baser Earth didst make,
And who with Eden didst devise the Snake;
    For all the Sin where with the Face of Man
Is blacken'd, Man's Forgiveness give—and take!

*   *   *   *   *   *   *   *

KÚZA-NÁMA

59

Listen again. One Evening at the Close
Of Ramazán, ere the better Moon arose,
    In that old Potter's Shop I stood alone
With the clay Population round in Rows.

60

And, strange to tell, among that Earthen Lot
Some could articulate, while others not:
    And suddenly one more impatient cried—
"Who *is* the Potter, pray, and who the Pot?"

61

Then said another—"Surely not in vain
"My Substance from the common Earth was ta'en,
   "That He who subtly wrought me into Shape
"Should stamp me back to common Earth again."

62

Another said—"Why, ne'er a peevish Boy,
"Would break the Bowl from which he drank in Joy;
   "Shall He that *made* the Vessel in pure Love
"And Fancy, in an after Rage destroy!"

63

None answer'd this; but after Silence spake
A Vessel of a more ungainly Make:
   "They sneer at me for leaning all awry;
"What! did the Hand then of the Potter shake?"

64

Said one—"Folks of a surly Tapster tell,
"And daub his Visage with the Smoke of Hell;
   "They talk of some strict Testing of us—Pish!
"He's a Good Fellow, and 'twill all be well."

65

Then said another with a long-drawn Sigh,
"My Clay with long oblivion is gone dry:
   "But, fill me with the old familiar Juice,
"Methinks I might recover by-and-bye!"

66

So while the Vessels one by one were speaking,
One spied the little Crescent all were seeking:[30]
　　And then they jogg'd each other, "Brother! Brother!
"Hark to the Porter's Shoulder-knot a-creaking!"

*　*　*　*　*　*　*　*

67

Ah, with the Grape my fading Life provide,
And wash my Body whence the Life has died,
　　And in a Windingsheet of Vine-leaf wrapt,
So bury me by some sweet Garden-side.

68

That ev'n my buried Ashes such a Snare
Of Perfume shall fling up into the Air,
　　As not a True Believer passing by
But shall be overtaken unaware.

69

Indeed the Idols I have loved so long
Have done my Credit in Men's Eye much wrong;
　　Have drown'd my Honour in a shallow Cup,
And sold my Reputation for a Song.

70

Indeed, indeed, Repentance oft before
I swore—but was I sober when I swore?
　　And then and then came Spring, and Rose-in-hand
My thread-bare Penitence apieces tore.

71

And much as Wine has play'd the Infidel,
And robb'd me of my Robe of Honour—well,
   I often wonder what the Vintners buy
One half so precious as the Goods they sell.

72

Alas, that Spring should vanish with the Rose!
That Youth's sweet-scented Manuscript should close!
   The Nightingale that in the Branches sang,
Ah, whence, and whither flown again, who knows!

73

Ah Love! could thou and I with Fate conspire
To grasp this sorry Scheme of Things entire,
   Would not we shatter it to bits—and then
Re-mould it nearer to the Heart's Desire!

74

Ah, Moon of my Delight who know'st no wane,
The Moon of Heav'n is rising once again:
   How oft hereafter rising shall she look
Through this same Garden after me—in vain!

75

And when Thyself with shining Foot shall pass
Among the Guests Star-scatter'd on the Grass,
   And in thy joyous Errand reach the Spot
Where I made one—turn down an empty Glass!

TAMÁM SHUD

Second Edition (1868)

1

Wake! For the Sun behind yon Eastern height
Has chased the Session of the Stars from Night;
   And, to the field of Heav'n ascending, strikes
The Sultán's Turret with a Shaft of Light.

2

Before the phantom of False morning died,[2]
Methought a Voice within the Tavern cried,
   "When all the Temple is prepared within,
"Why lags the drowsy Worshipper outside?"

3

And, as the Cock crew, those who stood before
The Tavern shouted—"Open then the door!
   "You know how little while we have to stay,
"And once departed, may return no more."

4

Now the New Year reviving old Desires,[3]
The thoughtful Soul to Solitude retires,
   Where the WHITE HAND OF MOSES on the Bough
Puts out, and Jesus from the Ground suspires.[4]

5

Iram indeed is gone with all his Rose,[5]
And Jamshýd's Sev'n-ring'd Cup where no one knows;
   But still a Ruby gushes from the Vine,
And many a Garden by the Water blows.

6

And David's lips are lockt; but in divine[6]
High-piping Péhlevi, with "Wine! Wine! Wine!
    "Red Wine!"—the Nightingale cries to the Rose
That sallow cheek[7] of her's to incarnadine.

7

Come, fill the Cup, and in the fire of Spring
Your Winter-garment of Repentance fling:
    The Bird of Time has but a little way
To flutter—and the Bird is on the Wing.

8 #

Whether at Naishápúr or Babylon,
Whether the Cup with sweet or bitter run,
    The Wine of Life keeps oozing drop by drop,
The Leaves of Life keep falling one by one.

9

Morning a thousand Roses brings, you say;
Yes, but where leaves the Rose of yesterday?
    And this first Summer month that brings the Rose
Shall take Jamshýd and Kaikobád away.

10

Well, let it take them! What have we to do
With Kaikobád the Great, or Kaikhosrú?
    Let Rustum cry "To Battle!" as he likes,[8]
Or Hátim Tai "To Supper!"—heed not you.

11

With me along the strip of Herbage strown
That just divides the desert from the sown,
    Where name of Slave and Sultán is forgot—
And Peace to Máhmúd on his golden Throne!

12

Here with a little Bread beneath the Bough,
A Flask of Wine, a Book of Verse—and Thou
    Beside me singing in the Wilderness—
Oh, Wilderness were Paradise enow!

13

Some for the Glories of This World; and some
Sigh for the Prophet's Paradise to come;
    Ah, take the Cash, and let the Promise go,
Nor heed the music of a distant Drum![9]

14 # Ø

Were it not Folly, Spider-like to spin
The Thread of present life away to win—
    What? for ourselves, who know not if we shall
Breathe out the very Breath we now breathe in!

15

Look to the blowing Rose about us—"Lo,
"Laughing," she says, "into the world I blow:
    "At once the silken tassel of my Purse
"Tear, and its Treasure on the Garden throw."[10]

16

For those who husbanded the Golden grain,
And those who flung it to the winds like Rain,
    Alike to no such aureate Earth are turn'd
As, buried once, Men want dug up again.

17

The Worldly Hope men set their Hearts upon
Turns Ashes—or it prospers; and anon,
    Like Snow upon the Desert's dusty Face,
Lighting a little hour or two—was gone.

18

Think, in this batter'd Caravanserai
Whose Portals are alternate Night and Day,
    How Sultán after Sultán with his Pomp
Abode his destin'd Hour, and went his way.

19

They say the Lion and the Lizard keep
The Courts where Jamshýd gloried and drank deep:[11]
    And Bahrám, that great Hunter—the Wild Ass[12]
Stamps o'er his Head, but cannot break his Sleep.

20 # Ø

The Palace that to Heav'n his pillars threw,
And Kings the forehead on his threshold drew—
    I saw the solitary Ringdove there,
And "Coo, coo, coo," she cried; and "Coo, coo, coo."[13]

21

Ah, my Belovéd, fill the Cup that clears
To-DAY of past Regret and future Fears:
    To-morrow!—Why, To-morrow I may be
Myself with Yesterday's Sev'n thousand Years.[15]

22

For some we loved, the loveliest and the best
That from his Vintage rolling Time has prest,
    Have drunk their Cup a Round or two before,
And one by one crept silently to rest.

23

And we, that now make merry in the Room
They left, and Summer dresses in new bloom,
    Ourselves must we beneath the Couch of Earth
Descend, ourselves to make a Couch—for whom?

24

I sometimes think that never blows so red
The Rose as where some buried Caesar bled;
    That every Hyacinth the Garden wears
Dropt in her Lap from some once lovely Head.

25

And this delightful Herb whose living Green
Fledges the River's Lip on which we lean—
    Ah, lean upon it lightly! for who knows
From what once lovely Lip it springs unseen!

26

Ah, make the most of what we yet may spend,
Before we too into the Dust descend;
    Dust into Dust, and under Dust, to lie,
Sans Wine, sans Song, sans Singer, and—sans End!

27

Alike for those who for To-DAY prepare,
And those that after some To-MORROW stare,
    A Muezzín from the Tower of Darkness cries,
"Fools! your Reward is neither Here nor There!"

28 # Ø

Another Voice, when I am sleeping, cries,
"The Flower should open with the Morning skies."
    And a retreating Whisper, as I wake—
"The Flower that once has blown for ever dies."

29

Why, all the Saints and Sages who discuss'd
Of the Two Worlds so learnedly, are thrust
    Like foolish Prophets forth; their Words to Scorn
Are scatter'd, and their Mouths are stopt with Dust.

30

Myself when young did eagerly frequent
Doctor and Saint, and heard great argument
    About it and about: but evermore
Came out by the same door as in I went.

31

With them the seed of Wisdom did I sow,
And with mine own hand wrought to make it grow:
    And this was all the Harvest that I reap'd—
"I came like Water, and like Wind I go."

32

Into this Universe, and *Why* not knowing,
Nor *Whence*, like Water willy-nilly flowing:
    And out of it, as Wind along the Waste,
I know not *Whither*, willy-nilly blowing.

33

What, without asking, hither hurried *Whence*?
And, without asking, *Whither* hurried hence!
    Ah, contrite Heav'n endowed us with the Vine
To drug the memory of that insolence!

34

Up from Earth's Centre through the Seventh Gate
I rose, and on the Throne of Saturn sate,[16]
    And many Knots unravel'd by the Road;
But not the Master-knot of Human Fate.

35

There was the Door to which I found no Key:
There was the Veil through which I could not see:
    Some little talk awhile of ME and THEE
There was—and then no more of THEE and ME.[17]

36 #

Earth could not answer; nor the Seas that mourn
In flowing Purple, of their Lord forlorn;
    Nor Heaven, with those eternal Signs reveal'd
And hidden by the sleeve of Night and Morn.

37

Then of the THEE IN ME who works behind
The Veil of Universe I cried to find
    A Lamp to guide me through the darkness; and
Something then said—"An Understanding blind."

38

Then to the Lip of this poor earthen Urn
I lean'd, the secret Well of Life to learn:
    And Lip to Lip it murmur'd—"While you live,
"Drink!—for, once dead, you never shall return."

39

I think the Vessel, that with fugitive
Articulation answer'd, once did live,
    And drink; and that impassive Lip I kiss'd,
How many Kisses might it take—and give!

40

For I remember stopping by the way
To watch a Potter thumping his wet Clay:
    And with its all-obliterated Tongue
It murmur'd—"Gently, Brother, gently, pray!"

41 #

For has not such a Story from of Old
Down Man's successive generations roll'd
   Of such a clod of saturated Earth
Cast by the Maker into Human mould?

42 #

And not a drop that from our Cups we throw[19]
On the parcht herbage but may steal below
   To quench the fire of Anguish in some Eye
There hidden—far beneath, and long ago.

43 #

As then the Tulip for her wonted sup
Of Heavenly Vintage lifts her chalice up,
   Do you, twin offspring of the soil, till Heav'n
To Earth invert you like an empty Cup.

44 # Ø

Do you, within your little hour of Grace,
The waving Cypress in your Arms enlace,
   Before the Mother back into her arms
Fold, and dissolve you in a last embrace.

45

And if the Cup you drink, the Lip you press,
End in what All begins and ends in—Yes;
   Imagine then you *are* what heretofore
You *were*—hereafter you shall not be less.

46

So when at last the Angel of the drink[20]
Of Darkness finds you by the river-brink,
   And, proffering his Cup, invites your Soul
Forth to your Lips to quaff it—do not shrink.

47

And fear not lest Existence closing *your*
Account, should lose, or know the type no more;
   The Eternal Sáki from that Bowl has pour'd
Millions of Bubbles like us, and will pour.

48

When You and I behind the Veil are past,
Oh but the long long while the World shall last,
   Which of our Coming and Departure heeds
As much as Ocean of a pebble-cast.

49

One Moment in Annihilation's Waste,
One Moment, of the Well of Life to taste—
   The Stars are setting, and the Caravan[21]
Draws to the Dawn of Nothing—Oh make haste!

50

Would you that spangle of Existence spend
About THE SECRET—quick about it, Friend!
   A Hair, they say, divides the False and True—
And upon what, prithee, does Life depend?

51

A Hair, they say, divides the False and True;
Yes; and a single Alif were the clue,
   Could you but find it, to the Treasure-house,
And peradventure to THE MASTER too;

52

Whose secret Presence, through Creation's veins
Running, Quicksilver-like eludes your pains:
   Taking all shapes from Máh to Máhi;[22] and
They change and perish all—but He remains;

53

A moment guess'd—then back behind the Fold
Immerst of Darkness round the Drama roll'd
   Which, for the Pastime of Eternity,
He doth Himself contrive, enact, behold.

54

But if in vain, down on the stubborn floor
Of Earth, and up to Heav'n's unopening Door,
   You gaze To-day, while You are You—how then
To-morrow, You when shall be You no more?

55

Oh, plagued no more with Human or Divine,
To-morrow's tangle to itself resign,
   And lose your fingers in the tresses of
The Cypress-slender Minister of Wine.

56

Waste not your Hour, nor in the vain pursuit
Of This and That endeavour and dispute;
   Better be merry with the fruitful Grape
Than sadden after none, or bitter, Fruit.

57

You know, my Friends, how bravely in my House
For a new Marriage I did make Carouse:
   Divorced old barren Reason from my Bed,
And took the Daughter of the Vine to Spouse.

58

For "Is" and "Is-NOT" though with Rule and Line,[23]
And "Up-AND-DOWN" by Logic I define,
   Of all that one should care to fathom, I
Was never deep in anything but—Wine.

59

Ah, but my Computations, People say,
Have squared the Year to human compass, eh?
   If so, by striking from the Calendar
Unborn To-morrow, and dead Yesterday.

60

And lately, by the Tavern Door agape,
Came shining through the Dusk an Angel Shape
   Bearing a Vessel on his Shoulder; and
He bid me taste of it; and 'twas—the Grape!

61

The Grape that can with Logic absolute
The Two-and-Seventy jarring Sects confute:[24]
   The sovereign Alchemist that in a trice
Life's leaden metal into Gold transmute:

62

The mighty Mahmúd, Allah-breathing Lord,
That all the misbelieving and black Horde[25]
   Of Fears and Sorrows that infest the Soul
Scatters before him with his whirlwind Sword.

63 #

Why, be this Juice the growth of God, who dare
Blaspheme the twisted tendril as a Snare?
   A Blessing, we should use it, should we not?
And if a Curse—why, then, Who set it there?

64 #

I must abjure the Balm of Life, I must,
Scared by some After-reckoning ta'en on trust,
   Or lured with Hope of some Diviner Drink,
When the frail Cup is crumbled into Dust!

65 # Ø

If but the Vine and Love-abjuring Band
Are in the Prophet's Paradise to stand,
   Alack, I doubt the Prophet's Paradise
Were empty as the hollow of one's Hand.

66

Oh threats of Hell and Hopes of Paradise!
One thing at least is certain—*This* Life flies:
    One thing is certain and the rest is lies;
The Flower that once is blown for ever dies.

67 #

Strange, is it not? that of the myriads who
Before us pass'd the door of Darkness through
    Not one returns to tell us of the Road,
Which to discover we must travel too.

68 #

The Revelations of Devout and Learn'd
Who rose before us, and as Prophets burn'd,
    Are all but Stories, which, awoke from Sleep
They told their fellows, and to Sleep return'd.

69 #

Why, if the Soul can fling the Dust aside,
And naked on the Air of Heaven ride,
    Is't not a shame—is't not a shame for him
So long in this Clay suburb to abide!

70 #

But that is but a Tent wherein may rest
A Sultan to the realm of Death addrest;
    The Sultan rises, and the dark Ferrásh
Strikes, and prepares it for another guest.

71 #

I sent my Soul through the Invisible,
Some letter of that After-life to spell:
    And after many days my Soul return'd
And said, "Behold, Myself am Heav'n and Hell:"

72 #

Heav'n but the Vision of fulfill'd Desire,
And Hell the Shadow of a Soul on fire,
    Cast on the Darkness into which Ourselves,
So late emerg'd from, shall so soon expire.

73

We are no other than a moving row
Of visionary Shapes that come and go
    Round with this Sun-illumin'd Lantern held
In Midnight by the Master of the Show;[26]

74

Impotent Pieces of the Game He plays
Upon this Chequer-board of Nights and Days;
    Hither and thither moves, and checks, and slays;
And one by one back in the Closet lays.

75

The Ball no question makes of Ayes and Noes,
But Right or Left as strikes the Player goes;
    And He that toss'd you down into the Field,
He knows about it all—HE knows—HE knows![27]

76

The Moving Finger writes; and, having writ,
Moves on: nor all your Piety nor Wit
    Shall lure it back to cancel half a Line,
Nor all your Tears wash out a Word of it.

77 # Ø

For let Philosopher and Doctor preach
Of what they will, and what they will not—each
    Is but one Link in an eternal Chain
That none can slip, nor break, nor over-reach.

78

And that inverted Bowl we call The Sky,
Whereunder crawling coop'd we live and die,
    Lift not your hands to *It* for help—for It
As impotently rolls as you or I.

79

With Earth's first Clay They did the Last Man knead,
And there of the Last Harvest sow'd the Seed:
    And the first Morning of Creation wrote
What the Last Dawn of Reckoning shall read.

80

Yesterday *This* Day's Madness did prepare;
To-morrow's Silence, Triumph, or Despair:
    Drink! for you know not whence you came, nor why:
Drink! for you know not why you go, nor where.

81

I tell you this—When, started from the Goal,
Over the flaming shoulders of the Foal
   Of Heav'n Parwín and Mushtari they flung,[28]
In my predestin'd Plot of Dust and Soul

82

The Vine had struck a fibre: which about
If clings my Being—let the Dervish flout;
   Of my Base metal may be filed a Key,
That shall unlock the Door he howls without.

83

And this I know: whether the one True Light,
Kindle to Love, or Wrath-consume me quite,
   One flash of It within the Tavern caught
Better than in the Temple lost outright.

84

What! Out of senseless Nothing to provoke
A conscious Something to resent the yoke
   Of unpermitted Pleasure, under pain
Of Everlasting Penalties, if broke!

85

What! from his helpless Creature be repaid
Pure Gold for what he lent us dross-allay'd—
   Sue for a Debt we never did contract,
And cannot answer—Oh the sorry trade!

86 # Ø

Nay, but, for terror of his wrathful Face,
I swear I will not call Injustice Grace;
   Not one Good Fellow of the Tavern but
Would kick so poor a Coward from the place.

87

Oh Thou, who didst with pitfall and with gin
Beset the Road I was to wander in,
   Thou wilt not with Predestin'd Evil round
Enmesh, and then impute my Fall to Sin?

88

Oh Thou, who Man of baser Earth didst make,
And ev'n with Paradise devise the Snake:
   For all the Sin the Face of wretched Man
Is black with—Man's Forgiveness give—and take!

*   *   *   *   *

89

As under cover of departing Day
Slunk hunger-stricken Ramazán away,
   Once more within the Potter's house alone
I stood, surrounded by the Shapes of Clay.

90

And once again there gather'd a scarce heard
Whisper among them; as it were, the stirr'd
   Ashes of some all but extinguisht Tongue,
Which mine ear kindled into living Word.

91

Said one among them—"Surely not in vain,
"My Substance from the common Earth was ta'en,
   "That He who subtly wrought me into Shape
"Should stamp me back to shapeless Earth again?"

92

Another said—"Why, ne'er a peevish Boy
"Would break the Cup from which he drank in Joy;
   "Shall He that of his own free Fancy made
"The Vessel, in an after-rage destroy!"

93

None answer'd this; but after silence spake
Some Vessel of a more ungainly Make;
   "They sneer at me for leaning all awry;
"What! did the Hand then of the Potter shake?"

94

Thus with the Dead as with the Living, *What?*
And *Why?* so ready, but the *Wherefor* not,
   One on a sudden peevishly exclaim'd,
"Which is the Potter, pray, and which the Pot?"

95

Said one—"Folks of a surly Master tell,
"And daub his Visage with the Smoke of Hell;
   "They talk of some sharp Trial of us—Pish!
"He's a Good Fellow, and 'twill all be well."

96

"Well," said another, "Whoso will, let try,
"My Clay with long oblivion is gone dry:
    "But, fill me with the old familiar Juice,
"Methinks I might recover by-and-bye!"

97

So while the Vessels one by one were speaking,
One spied the little Crescent all were seeking:[30]
    And then they jogg'd each other, "Brother! Brother!
"Now for the Porter's shoulder-knot a-creaking!"

*   *   *   *   *

98

Ah, with the Grape my fading Life provide,
And wash my Body whence the Life has died,
    And lay me, shrouded in the living Leaf,
By some not unfrequented Garden-side.

99 # Ø

Whither resorting from the vernal Heat
Shall Old Acquaintance Old Acquaintance greet,
    Under the Branch that leans above the Wall
To shed his Blossom over head and feet.

100

Then ev'n my buried Ashes such a snare
Of Vintage shall fling up into the Air,
    As not a True-believer passing by
But shall be overtaken unaware.

101

Indeed the Idols I have loved so long
Have done my credit in Men's eye much wrong:
   Have drown'd my Glory in a shallow Cup,
And sold my Reputation for a Song.

102

Indeed, indeed, Repentance oft before
I swore—but was I sober when I swore?
   And then and then came Spring, and Rose-in-hand
My thread-bare Penitence apieces tore.

103

And much as Wine has play'd the Infidel,
And robb'd me of my Robe of Honour—Well,
   I often wonder what the Vintners buy
One half so precious as the ware they sell.

104

Yet Ah, that Spring should vanish with the Rose!
That Youth's sweet-scented manuscript should close!
   The Nightingale that in the branches sang,
Ah whence, and whither flown again, who knows!

105

Would but the Desert of the Fountain yield
One glimpse—if dimly, yet indeed, reveal'd,
   Toward which the fainting Traveller might spring,
As springs the trampled herbage of the field!

106

Oh if the World were but to re-create,
That we might catch ere closed the Book of Fate,
    And make The Writer on a fairer leaf
Inscribe our names, or quite obliterate!

107 # Ø

Better, oh better, cancel from the Scroll
Of Universe one luckless Human Soul,
    Than drop by drop enlarge the Flood that rolls
Hoarser with Anguish as the Ages roll.

108

Ah Love! could you and I with Fate conspire
To grasp this sorry Scheme of Things entire,
    Would not we shatter it to bits—and then
Re-mould it nearer to the Heart's Desire!

109

But see! The rising Moon of Heav'n again
Looks for us, Sweet-heart, through the quivering Plane:
    How oft hereafter rising will she look
Among those leaves—for one of us in vain!

110

And when Yourself with silver Foot shall pass
Among the Guests Star-scatter'd on the Grass,
    And in your joyous errand reach the spot
Where I made One—turn down an empty Glass!

TAMÁM

Fourth Edition (1879)

1

WAKE! For the Sun who scatter'd into flight
The Stars before him from the Field of Night,
   Drives Night along with them from Heav'n, and strikes
The Sultán's Turret with a Shaft of Light.

2

Before the phantom of False morning died,[2]
Methought a Voice within the Tavern cried,
   "When all the Temple is prepared within,
"Why nods the drowsy Worshipper outside?"

3

And, as the Cock crew, those who stood before
The Tavern shouted—"Open then the Door!
   "You know how little while we have to stay,
"And, once departed, may return no more."

4

Now the New Year reviving old Desires,[3]
The thoughtful Soul to Solitude retires,
   Where the WHITE HAND OF MOSES on the Bough
Puts out, and Jesus from the Ground suspires.[4]

5

Iram indeed is gone with all his Rose,[5]
And Jamshyd's Sev'n-ring'd Cup where no one knows;
   But still a Ruby kindles in the Vine,
And many a Garden by the Water blows.

6

And David's lips are lockt; but in divine[6]
High-piping Pehleví, with "Wine! Wine! Wine!
    "Red Wine!"—the Nightingale cries to the Rose
That sallow cheek[7] of her's to' incarnadine.

7

Come, fill the Cup, and in the fire of Spring
Your Winter-garment of Repentance fling:
    The Bird of Time has but a little way
To flutter—and the Bird is on the Wing.

8

Whether at Naishápúr or Babylon,
Whether the Cup with sweet or bitter run,
    The Wine of Life keeps oozing drop by drop,
The Leaves of Life keep falling one by one.

9

Each Morn a thousand Roses brings, you say;
Yes, but where leaves the Rose of Yesterday?
    And this first Summer month that brings the Rose
Shall take Jamshyd and Kaikobád away.

10

Well, let it take them! What have we to do
With Kaikobád the Great, or Kaikhosrú?
    Let Zál and Rustum bluster as they will,[8]
Or Hátim call to Supper—heed not you.

11

With me along the strip of Herbage strown
That just divides the desert from the sown,
    Where name of Slave and Sultán is forgot—
And Peace to Mahmúd on his golden Throne!

12

A Book of Verses underneath the Bough,
A Jug of Wine, a Loaf of Bread—and Thou
    Beside me singing in the Wilderness—
Oh, Wilderness were Paradise enow!

13

Some for the Glories of This World; and some
Sigh for the Prophet's Paradise to come;
    Ah, take the Cash, and let the Credit go,
Nor heed the rumble of a distant Drum![9]

14

Look to the blowing Rose about us—"Lo,
"Laughing," she says, "into the world I blow,
    "At once the silken tassel of my Purse
"Tear, and its Treasure on the Garden throw."[10]

15

And those who husbanded the Golden Grain,
And those who flung it to the winds like Rain,
    Alike to no such aureate Earth are turn'd
As, buried once, Men want dug up again.

16

The Worldly Hope men set their Hearts upon
Turns Ashes—or it prospers; and anon,
    Like Snow upon the Desert's dusty Face,
Lighting a little hour or two—was gone.

17

Think, in this batter'd Caravanserai
Whose Portals are alternate Night and Day,
    How Sultán after Sultán with his Pomp
Abode his Destin'd Hour, and went his way.

18

They say the Lion and the Lizard keep
The Courts where Jamshyd gloried and drank deep:[11] [13]
    And Bahrám, that great Hunter—the Wild Ass[12]
Stamps o'er his Head, but cannot break his Sleep.

19

I sometimes think that never blows so red
The Rose as where some buried Caesar bled;[14]
    That every Hyacinth the Garden wears
Dropt in her Lap from some once lovely Head.

20

And this reviving Herb whose tender Green
Fledges the River-Lip on which we lean—
    Ah, lean upon it lightly! for who knows
From what once lovely Lip it springs unseen!

21

Ah, my Belovéd, fill the Cup that clears
To-DAY of past Regret and future Fears:
   To-morrow!—why, To-morrow I may be
Myself with Yesterday's Sev'n thousand Years.[15]

22

For some we loved, the loveliest and the best
That from his Vintage rolling Time hath prest,
   Have drunk their Cup a Round or two before,
And one by one crept silently to rest.

23

And we, that now make merry in the Room
They left, and Summer dresses in new bloom,
   Ourselves must we beneath the Couch of Earth
Descend—ourselves to make a Couch—for whom?

24

Ah, make the most of what we yet may spend,
Before we too into the Dust descend;
   Dust into Dust, and under Dust, to lie,
Sans Wine, sans Song, sans Singer, and—sans End!

25

Alike for those who for To-DAY prepare,
And those that after some To-MORROW stare,
   A Muezzín from the Tower of Darkness cries,
"Fools! your Reward is neither Here nor There."

26

Why, all the Saints and Sages who discuss'd
Of the Two Worlds so wisely—they are thrust
   Like foolish Prophets forth; their Words to Scorn
Are scatter'd, and their Mouths are stopt with Dust.

27

Myself when young did eagerly frequent
Doctor and Saint, and heard great argument
   About it and about: but evermore
Came out by the same door where in I went.

28

With them the seed of Wisdom did I sow,
And with mine own hand wrought to make it grow;
   And this was all the Harvest that I reap'd—
"I came like Water, and like Wind I go."

29

Into this Universe, and *Why* not knowing
Nor *Whence*, like Water willy-nilly flowing;
   And out of it, as Wind along the Waste,
I know not *Whither*, willy-nilly blowing.

30

What, without asking, hither hurried *Whence?*
And, without asking, *Whither* hurried hence!
   Oh, many a Cup of this forbidden Wine
Must drown the memory of that insolence!

31

Up from Earth's Centre through the Seventh Gate
I rose, and on the Throne of Saturn sate,[16]
   And many a Knot unravel'd by the Road;
But not the Master-knot of Human Fate.

32

There was the Door to which I found no Key;
There was the Veil through which I might not see
   Some little talk awhile of ME and THEE
There was—and then no more of THEE and ME.[17]

33

Earth could not answer; nor the Seas that mourn
In flowing Purple, of their Lord forlorn;
   Nor rolling Heaven, with all his Signs reveal'd
And hidden by the sleeve of Night and Morn.

34

Then of the THEE IN ME who works behind
The Veil, I lifted up my hands to find
   A lamp amid the Darkness; and I heard,
As from Without—"THE ME WITHIN THEE BLIND!"

35

Then to the Lip of this poor earthen Urn
I lean'd, the Secret of my Life to learn:
   And Lip to Lip it murmur'd—"While you live,
"Drink!—for, once dead, you never shall return."

36

I think the Vessel, that with fugitive
Articulation answer'd, once did live,
   And drink; and Ah! the passive Lip I kiss'd,
How many Kisses might it take—and give!

37

For I remember stopping by the way
To watch a Potter thumping his wet Clay:
   And with its all-obliterated Tongue
It murmur'd—"Gently, Brother, gently, pray!"[18]

38

And has not such a Story from of Old
Down Man's successive generations roll'd
   Of such a clod of saturated Earth
Cast by the Maker into Human mould?

39

And not a drop that from our Cups we throw[19]
For Earth to drink of, but may steal below
   To quench the fire of Anguish in some Eye
There hidden—far beneath, and long ago.

40

As then the Tulip for her morning sup
Of Heav'nly Vintage from the soil looks up,
   Do you devoutly do the like, till Heav'n
To Earth invert you—like an empty Cup.

41

Perplext no more with Human or Divine,
To-morrow's tangle to the winds resign,
    And lose your fingers in the tresses of
The Cypress-slender Minister of Wine.

42

And if the Wine you drink, the Lip you press,
End in what All begins and ends in—Yes;
    Think then you are To-day what Yesterday
You were—To-morrow you shall not be less.

43

So when the Angel of the darker Drink [20]
At last shall find you by the river-brink,
    And, offering his Cup, invite your Soul
Forth to your Lips to quaff—you shall not shrink.

44

Why, if the Soul can fling the Dust aside,
And naked on the Air of Heaven ride,
    Wer't not a Shame—wer't not a Shame for him
In this clay carcase crippled to abide?

45

'Tis but a Tent where takes his one day's rest
A Sultán to the realm of Death addrest;
    The Sultán rises, and the dark Ferrásh
Strikes, and prepares it for another Guest.

46

And fear not lest Existence closing your
Account, and mine, should know the like no more;
　　The Eternal Sákí from that Bowl has pour'd
Millions of Bubbles like us, and will pour.

47

When You and I behind the Veil are past,
Oh, but the long, long while the World shall last,
　　Which of our Coming and Departure heeds
As the Sea's self should heed a pebble-cast.

48

A Moment's Halt—a momentary taste
Of BEING from the Well amid the Waste—
　　And Lo!—the phantom Caravan has reacht
The NOTHING it set out from—Oh, make haste!

49

Would you that spangle of Existence spend
About THE SECRET—quick about it, Friend!
　　A Hair perhaps divides the False and True—
And upon what, prithee, does life depend?

50

A Hair perhaps divides the False and True
Yes; and a single Alif were the clue—
　　Could you but find it—to the Treasure-house,
And peradventure to THE MASTER too;

51

Whose secret Presence, through Creation's veins
Running Quicksilver-like eludes your pains;
   Taking all shapes from Máh to Máhi;[22] and
They change and perish all—but He remains;

52

A moment guess'd—then back behind the Fold
Immerst of Darkness round the Drama roll'd
   Which, for the Pastime of Eternity,
He doth Himself contrive, enact, behold.

53

But if in vain, down on the stubborn floor
Of Earth, and up to Heav'n's unopening Door,
   You gaze TO-DAY, while You are You—how then
TO-MORROW, You when shall be You no more?

54

Waste not your Hour, nor in the vain pursuit
Of This and That endeavour and dispute;
   Better be jocund with the fruitful Grape
Than sadden after none, or bitter, Fruit.

55

You know, my Friends, with what a brave Carouse
I made a Second Marriage in my house;
   Divorced old barren Reason from my Bed,
And took the Daughter of the Vine to Spouse.

56

For "Is" and "Is-NOT" though with Rule and Line,[23]
And "UP-AND-DOWN" by Logic I define,
    Of all that one should care to fathom, I
Was never deep in anything but—Wine.

57

Ah, but my Computations, People say,
Reduced the Year to better reckoning?—Nay,
    'Twas only striking from the Calendar
Unborn To-morrow, and dead Yesterday.

58

And lately, by the Tavern Door agape,
Came shining through the Dusk an Angel Shape
    Bearing a Vessel on his Shoulder; and
He bid me taste of it; and 'twas—the Grape!

59

The Grape that can with Logic absolute
The Two-and-Seventy jarring Sects confute:[24]
    The sovereign Alchemist that in a trice
Life's leaden metal into Gold transmute:

60

The mighty Mahmúd, Allah-breathing Lord,
That all the misbelieving and black Horde[25]
    Of Fears and Sorrows that infest the Soul
Scatters before him with his whirlwind Sword.

61

Why, be this Juice the growth of God, who dare
Blaspheme the twisted tendril as a Snare?
    A Blessing, we should use it, should we not?
And if a Curse—why, then, Who set it there?

62

I must abjure the Balm of Life, I must,
Scared by some After-reckoning ta'en on trust,
    Or lured with Hope of some Diviner Drink,
To fill the Cup—when crumbled into Dust!

63

Oh threats of Hell and Hopes of Paradise!
One thing at least is certain—*This* Life flies;
    One thing is certain and the rest is Lies;
The Flower that once has blown for ever dies.

64

Strange, is it not? that of the myriads who
Before us pass'd the door of Darkness through,
    Not one returns to tell us of the Road,
Which to discover we must travel too.

65

The Revelations of Devout and Learn'd
Who rose before us, and as Prophets burn'd,
    Are all but Stories, which, awoke from Sleep
They told their comrades, and to Sleep return'd.

66

I sent my Soul through the Invisible,
Some letter of that After-life to spell:
    And by and by my Soul return'd to me,
And answer'd "I Myself am Heav'n and Hell:"

67

Heav'n but the Vision of fulfill'd Desire,
And Hell the Shadow from a Soul on fire
    Cast on the Darkness into which Ourselves,
So late emerg'd from, shall so soon expire.

68

We are no other than a moving row
Of Magic Shadow-shapes that come and go
    Round with the Sun-illumin'd Lantern held
In Midnight by the Master of the Show;[26]

69

But helpless Pieces of the Game He plays
Upon this Chequer-board of Nights and Days;
    Hither and thither moves, and checks, and slays,
And one by one back in the Closet lays.

70

The Ball no question makes of Ayes and Noes,
But Here or There as strikes the Player goes;
    And He that toss'd you down into the Field,
He knows about it all—HE knows—HE knows![27]

71

The Moving Finger writes; and, having writ,
Moves on: nor all your Piety nor Wit
   Shall lure it back to cancel half a Line,
Nor all your Tears wash out a Word of it.

72

And that inverted Bowl they call the Sky,
Whereunder crawling coop'd we live and die,
   Lift not your hands to *It* for help—for It
As impotently moves as you or I.

73

With Earth's first Clay They did the Last Man knead,
And there of the Last Harvest sow'd the Seed:
   And the first Morning of Creation wrote
What the Last Dawn of Reckoning shall read.

74

YESTERDAY *This* Day's Madness did prepare;
To-morrow's Silence, Triumph, or Despair:
   Drink! for you know not whence you came, nor why:
Drink! for you know not why you go, nor where.

75

I tell you this—When, started from the Goal,
Over the flaming shoulders of the Foal
   Of Heav'n Parwín and Mushtarí they flung,[28]
In my predestin'd Plot of Dust and Soul

76

The Vine had struck a fibre: which about
If clings my Being—let the Dervish flout;
    Of my Base metal may be filed a Key,
That shall unlock the Door he howls without.

77

And this I know: whether the one True Light
Kindle to Love, or Wrath-consume me quite,
    One Flash of It within the Tavern caught
Better than in the Temple lost outright.

78

What! out of senseless Nothing to provoke
A conscious Something to resent the yoke
    Of unpermitted Pleasure, under pain
Of Everlasting Penalties, if broke!

79

What! from his helpless Creature be repaid
Pure Gold for what he lent him dross-allay'd—
    Sue for a Debt we never did contract,
And cannot answer—Oh the sorry trade!

80

Oh Thou, who didst with pitfall and with gin
Beset the Road I was to wander in,
    Thou wilt not with Predestin'd Evil round
Enmesh, and then impute my Fall to Sin!

81

Oh Thou, who Man of baser Earth didst make,
And ev'n with Paradise devise the Snake:
    For all the Sin wherewith the Face of Man
Is blacken'd—Man's forgiveness give—and take!

*   *   *   *   *   *   *

82

As under cover of departing Day
Slunk hunger-stricken Ramazán away,
    Once more within the Potter's house alone
I stood, surrounded by the Shapes of Clay.

83

Shapes of all Sorts and Sizes, great and small,
That stood along the floor and by the wall;
    And some loquacious Vessels were; and some
Listen'd perhaps, but never talk'd at all.

84

Said one among them—"Surely not in vain
My substance of the common Earth was ta'en
    And to this Figure moulded, to be broke,
Or trampled back to shapeless Earth again."

85

Then said a Second—"Ne'er a peevish Boy
"Would break the Bowl from which he drank in joy;
    "And He that with his hand the Vessel made
"Will surely not in after Wrath destroy."

86

After a momentary silence spake
Some Vessel of a more ungainly Make;
    "They sneer at me for leaning all awry:
"What! did the Hand then of the Potter shake?"

87

Whereat some one of the loquacious Lot—
I think a Súfi pipkin—waxing hot—
    "All this of Pot and Potter—Tell me then,
"Who is the Potter, pray, and who the Pot?"[29]

88

"Why," said another, "Some there are who tell
"Of one who threatens he will toss to Hell
    "The luckless Pots he marr'd in making—Pish!
"He's a Good Fellow, and 't will all be well."

89

"Well," murmur'd one, "Let whoso make or buy,
"My Clay with long Oblivion is gone dry:
    "But fill me with the old familiar Juice,
"Methinks I might recover by and by."

90

So while the Vessels one by one were speaking,
The little Moon look'd in that all were seeking:[30]
    And then they jogg'd each other, "Brother! Brother!
"Now for the Porter's shoulder-knot a-creaking!"

*   *   *   *   *   *

91

Ah, with the Grape my fading Life provide,
And wash the Body whence the Life has died,
   And lay me, shrouded in the living Leaf,
By some not unfrequented Garden-side.

92

That ev'n my buried Ashes such a snare
Of Vintage shall fling up into the Air
   As not a True-believer passing by
But shall be overtaken unaware.

93

Indeed the Idols I have loved so long
Have done my credit in this World much wrong:
   Have drown'd my Glory in a shallow Cup,
And sold my Reputation for a Song.

94

Indeed, indeed, Repentance oft before
I swore—but was I sober when I swore?
   And then and then came Spring, and Rose-in-hand
My thread-bare Penitence apieces tore.

95

And much as Wine has play'd the Infidel,
And robb'd me of my Robe of Honour—Well,
   I wonder often what the Vintners buy
One half so precious as the stuff they sell.

96

Yet Ah, that Spring should vanish with the Rose!
That Youth's sweet-scented manuscript should close!
    The Nightingale that in the branches sang,
Ah whence, and whither flown again, who knows!

97

Would but the Desert of the Fountain yield
One glimpse—if dimly, yet indeed, reveal'd,
    To which the fainting Traveller might spring,
As springs the trampled herbage of the field!

98

Would but some wingéd Angel ere too late
Arrest the yet unfolded Roll of Fate,
    And make the stern Recorder otherwise
Enregister, or quite obliterate!

99

Ah Love! could you and I with Him conspire
To grasp this sorry Scheme of Things entire,
    Would not we shatter it to bits—and then
Re-mould it nearer to the Heart's Desire!

*   *   *   *   *   *

100

Yon rising Moon that looks for us again—
How oft hereafter will she wax and wane;
    How oft hereafter rising look for us
Through this same Garden—and for *one* in vain!

101

And when like her, oh Sákí, you shall pass
Among the Guests Star-scatter'd on the Grass,
    And in your joyous errand reach the spot
Where I made One—turn down an empty Glass!

TAMÁM

Edward FitzGerald's Notes

Composite text based mainly on the
Notes to the fourth edition (1879)

[1.] Flinging a Stone into the Cup was the Signal for "To Horse!" in the Desert. *[This note is only in first edition]*

[2.] The *"False Dawn;" Subhi Kázib*, a transient Light on the Horizon about an hour before the *Subhi sádik*, or True Dawn; a well known Phenomenon in the East.

[3.] New Year. Beginning with the Vernal Equinox, it must be remembered; and (howsoever the old Solar Year is practically superseded by the clumsy *Lunar* Year that dates from the Mohammedan Hijra) still commemorated by a Festival that is said to have been appointed by the very Jamshyd whom Omar so often talks of, and whose yearly Calendar he helped to rectify.

"The sudden approach and rapid advance of the Spring," says Mr. Binning, "are very striking. Before the Snow is well off the Ground, the Trees burst into Blossom, and the Flowers start from the Soil. At *Naw Rooz* (*their* New Year's Day) the Snow was lying in patches on the Hills and in the shaded Vallies, while the Fruit-trees in the Garden were budding beautifully, and green Plants and Flowers springing upon the Plains on every side—

> 'And on old Hyems' Chin and icy Crown
> 'An odorous Chaplet of sweet Summer buds
> 'Is, as in mockery, set—'—

Among the Plants newly appear'd I recognized some Acquaintances I had not seen for many a Year: among these, two varieties of the Thistle; a coarse species of the Daisy, like the Horse-gowan; red and white Clover; the Dock; the blue Corn-flower; and that vulgar Herb the Dandelion rearing its yellow crest on the Banks of the Water-courses." The Nightingale was not yet heard, for the Rose was not yet blown: but an almost identical Blackbird and Woodpecker helped to make up something of a North-country Spring.

[4.] "The White Hand of Moses." Exodus iv. 6; where Moses draws forth his Hand—not, according to the Persians, *"leprous as Snow,"*—but *white*, as our May-blossom in Spring perhaps. According to them also the Healing Power of Jesus resided in his Breath.

[5.] Iram, planted by King Shaddád, and now sunk somewhere in the Sands of Arabia. Jamshyd's Seven-ring'd Cup was typical of the 7 Heavens, 7 Planets, 7 Seas, &c., and was a *Divining Cup.*

[6.] *Pehlevi,* the old Heroic *Sanskrit* of Persia. Háfiz also speaks of the Nightingale's *Pehlevi,* which did not change with the People's.

[7.] I am not sure if the fourth line refers to the Red Rose looking sickly, or the Yellow Rose that ought to be Red; Red, White, and Yellow Roses all common in Persia. I think that Southey, in his Common-Place Book, quotes from some Spanish author about the Rose being White till 10 o'clock; "Rosa Perfecta" at 2; and "perfecta incarnada" at 5.

[8.] Rustum, the "Hercules" of Persia, and Zál his Father, whose exploits are among the most celebrated in the Sháh-náma. Hátim Tai, a well-known Type of Oriental Generosity.

[9.] A Drum—beaten outside a Palace.

[10.] That is, the Rose's Golden Centre.

[11.] Persepolis: call'd also *Takht-i-Jamshyd* —The Throne of Jamshyd, *"King Splendid,"* of the mythical *Peshdádian* Dynasty, and supposed (according to the Sháh-náma) to have been founded and built by him. Others refer it to the Work of the Genie King, Ján Ibn Ján—who also built the Pyramids—before the time of Adam. *[The following paragraph is only in first edition. It is based on Mr Binning's book mentioned in note 13 below and referenced on page 146.]*

It is also called *Chehl-minar—Forty-column*; which is Persian, probably, for *Column-countless*; the Hall they adorned or supported with their Lotus Base and taurine Capital indicating double that Number, though now counted down to less than half by Earthquake and other Inroad. By whomsoever built, unquestionably the Monument of a long extinguished Dynasty and Mythology; its Halls, Chambers and Galleries, inscribed with Arrow-head Characters, and sculptured with colossal, wing'd, half human Figures like those of Nimroud; Processions of Priests and Warriors—(doubtful if any where a Woman)—and Kings sitting on Thrones or in Chariots, Staff or Lotus-flower in hand, and the *Ferooher*—Symbol of Existence—with his wing'd Globe, common also to Assyria and Aegypt—over their heads. All this, together with Aqueduct and Cistern, and other Appurtenance of a Royal Palace, upon a Terrace-platform, ascended by a double Flight of Stairs that may be gallop'd up, and cut out of and into the Rock-side of the *Koh'i Ráhmet, Mountain of Mercy*, where the old Fire-worshiping Sovereigns are buried, and overlooking the Plain of Merdasht.

[12.] BAHRÁM GÚR.—*Bahram of the Wild Ass*—a Sassanian Sovereign—had also his Seven Castles (like the King of Bohemia!) each of a different Colour: each with a Royal Mistress within; each of whom tells him a Story, as told in one of the most famous Poems of Persia, written by Amír Khusraw: all these Sevens also figuring (according to Eastern Mysticism) the Seven Heavens; and perhaps the Book itself that Eighth, into which the mystical Seven transcend, and within which they revolve. The Ruins of Three of those Towers are yet shown by the Peasantry; as also the Swamp in which Bahrám sunk, like the Master of Ravenswood, while pursuing his *Gúr*.

[13.] *[The quatrain below was included in the notes to the first and fourth editions. It is quatrain 20 in the second edition.]*

> The Palace that to Heav'n his pillars threw,
> And Kings the forehead on his threshold drew—
>   I saw the solitary Ringdove there,
> And "Coo, coo, coo;" she cried; and "Coo, coo, coo."

This Quatrain Mr Binning found, among several of Háfiz and others, inscribed by some stray hand among the ruins of Persepolis. The Ringdove's ancient *Pehlevi, Coo, Coo, Coo,* signifies also in Persian *"Where? Where? Where?"* In Attár's "Bird-parliament" she is reproved by the Leader of the Birds for sitting still, and for ever harping on that one note of lamentation for her lost Yúsuf.

[14.] Apropos of Omar's Red Roses in Stanza XIX *[19 in the fourth edition]*, I am reminded of an old English Superstition, that our Anemone Pulsatilla, or purple "Pasque Flower," (which grows plentifully about the Fleam Dyke, near Cambridge), grows only where Danish Blood has been spilt. *[This note is only in fourth edition]*

[15.] A thousand years to each Planet.

[16.] Saturn, Lord of the Seventh Heaven.

[17.] ME-AND-THEE: some dividual Existence or Personality distinct from the Whole.

[18.] One of the Persian Poets—Attár, I think—has a pretty story about this. A thirsty Traveller dips his hand into a Spring of Water to drink from. By-and-by comes another who draws up and drinks from an earthen Bowl, and then departs, leaving his Bowl behind him. The first Traveller takes it up for another draught; but is surprised to find that the same Water which had tasted sweet from his own hand tastes bitter from the earthen Bowl. But a Voice— from Heaven, I think—tells him the clay from which the Bowl is made was once *Man;* and, into whatever shape renew'd, can never lose the bitter flavour of Mortality. *[This note is only in fourth edition]*

[19.] The custom of throwing a little Wine on the ground before drinking still continues in Persia, and perhaps generally in the East. Mons. Nicolas considers it "un signe de libéralité, et en même temps un avertissement que le buveur doit vider sa coupe jusqu'à la dernière goutte." *[a sign of liberality and at the same time a warning that the drinker should empty his cup down to the last drop.]* Is it not more likely an ancient Superstition; a Libation to propitiate Earth, or make her an Accomplice in the illicit Revel? Or, perhaps, to divert the Jealous Eye by some sacrifice of superfluity, as with the Ancients of the West? With Omar we see something more is signified; the precious Liquor is not lost, but sinks into the ground to refresh the dust of some poor Wine-worshipper foregone.

Thus Háfiz, copying Omar in so many ways: "When thou drinkest Wine pour a draught on the ground. Wherefore fear the Sin which brings to another Gain?" *[This note is not in first edition]*

[20.] According to one beautiful Oriental Legend, Azräel accomplishes his mission by holding to the nostril an Apple from the Tree of Life. *[This note is not in first edition; the following paragraph is only in fourth edition.]*

This, and the two following Stanzas would have been withdrawn, as somewhat *de trop,* from the Text, but for advice which I least like to disregard.

[21.] The Caravan travelling by Night (after their New Year's Day of the Vernal Equinox) by command of Mohammed, I believe. *[This note is not in fourth edition]*

[22.] From Máh to Máhi; from Fish to Moon. *[This note is not in first edition]*

[23.] A Jest, of course, at his Studies. A curious mathematical Quatrain of Omar's has been pointed out to me; the more curious because almost exactly parallel'd by some Verses of Doctor Donne's, that are quoted in Izaak Walton's Lives! Here is Omar: "You and I are the image of a pair of compasses; though we have two heads (sc. our *feet*) we have one body; when we have fixed the centre for our circle, we bring our heads (sc. feet) together at the end." Dr. Donne:

> If we be two, we two are so
>   As stiff twin-compassses are two;
> Thy Soul, the fixt foot, makes no show
>   To move, but does if the other do.

And though thine in the centre sit,
  Yet when my other far does roam,
Thine leans and hearkens after it,
  And grows erect as mine comes home.

Such thou must be to me, who must
  Like the other foot obliquely run;
Thy firmness makes my circle just,
  And me to end where I begun.

[24.] The Seventy-two Religions supposed to divide the World, *including* Islamism, as some think: but others not.

[25.] Alluding to Sultan Mahmúd's Conquest of India and its dark people.

[26.] *Fánúsi khiyál*, a Magic-lanthorn still used in India; the cylindrical Interior being painted with various Figures, and so lightly poised and ventilated as to revolve round the lighted Candle within.

[27.] A very mysterious Line in the original:

O dánad O dánad O dánad O——
[translated literally as 'He knows, he knows, he knows, he——']

breaking off something like our Wood-pigeon's Note, which she is said to take up just where she left off.

[28.] Parwín and Mushtarí—The Pleiads and Jupiter.

[29.] This Relation of Pot and Potter to Man and his Maker figures far and wide in the Literature of the World, from the time of the Hebrew Prophets to the present; when it may finally take the name of "Pot-theism," by which Mr. Carlyle ridiculed Sterling's "Pantheism." *My* Sheikh, whose knowledge flows in from all quarters, writes to me—

"Apropos of old Omar's Pots, did I ever tell you the sentence I found in 'Bishop Pearson on the Creed'? 'Thus are we wholly at the disposal of His will, and our present and future condition framed and ordered by His free, but wise and just, decrees. *Hath not the potter power over the clay, of the same lump to make one vessel unto honour, and another unto dishonour?* (Rom. ix, 21). And can that earth-artificer have a freer power over his *brother potsherd* (both being made of the same metal), than God hath over him, who, by the strange fecundity of His omnipotent power, first made the clay out of nothing, and then him out of that?'"

And again—from a very different quarter—"I had to refer the other day to Aristophanes, and came by chance on a curious Speaking-pot story in the Vespae, which I had quite forgotten.

[Here follows a piece of Greek text from Aristophanes' The Wasps (lines 1435–40), for which FitzGerald then gives an approximate translation as follows.]

"The Pot calls a bystander to be a witness to his bad treatment. The woman says, "If, by Proserpine, instead of all this 'testifying' (comp. Cuddie and his mother in 'Old Mortality!') you would buy yourself a rivet, it would show more sense in you!" The Scholiast explains *echinus* as ... *[Echinus is a Greek word translated above as 'pot'. FitzGerald then gives Greek text which means 'any bowl from the potter.']*

One more illustration for the oddity's sake from the "Autobiography of a Cornish Rector," by the late James Hamley Tregenna. 1871.

"There was one old Fellow in our Company—he was so like a Figure in the 'Pilgrim's Progress' that Richard always called him the 'ALLEGORY,' with a long white Beard—a rare Appendage in those days—and a Face the colour of which seemed to have been baked in, like the Faces one used to see on Earthenware Jugs. In our Country-dialect Earthenware is called *'Clome'*; so the Boys of the Village used to shout out after him—'Go back to the Potter, Old Clome-face, and get baked over again.' For the 'Allegory,' though shrewd enough in most things, had the reputation of being *'saift-baked,'* i.e., of weak intellect. *[This note is only in fourth edition]*

[30.] At the Close of the Fasting Month, Ramazán (which makes the Musulman unhealthy and unamiable), the first Glimpse of the New Moon (who rules their division of the Year), is looked for with the utmost Anxiety, and hailed with Acclamation. Then it is that the Porter's Knot may be heard—toward the *Cellar*. Omar has elsewhere a pretty Quatrain about the same Moon—

> "Be of Good Cheer—the sullen Month will die,
> "And a young Moon requite us by and by:
>   "Look how the Old one meagre, bent, and wan
> "With Age and Fast, is fainting from the Sky!"

FINIS

Edward FitzGerald's Prefaces

Composite text based mainly on the
Preface to the fourth edition (1879)

OMAR KHAYYÁM

THE

Astronomer-Poet of Persia

OMAR KHAYYÁM was born at Naishápúr in Khorasan in the latter half of our Eleventh, and died within the First Quarter of our Twelfth Century. The slender Story of his Life is curiously twined about that of two other very considerable Figures in their Time and Country: one of whom tells the Story of all Three. This was Nizám ul Mulk, Vizyr to Alp Arslan the Son, and Malik Shah the Grandson, of Toghrul Beg the Tartar, who had wrested Persia from the feeble Successor of Mahmúd the Great, and founded that Seljukian Dynasty which finally roused Europe into the Crusades. This Nizám ul Mulk, in his *Wasiyat*—or *Testament*—which he wrote and left as a Memorial for future Statesmen—relates the following, as quoted in the *Calcutta Review*, No. 59, from Mirkhond's History of the Assassins.

"'One of the greatest of the wise men of Khorassan was the Imám Mowaffak of Naishápúr, a man highly honoured and reverenced,—may God rejoice his soul; his illustrious years exceeded eighty-five, and it was the universal belief that every boy who read the Koran or studied the traditions in his presence, would assuredly attain to honour and happiness. For this cause did my father send me from Tús to Naishápúr with Abd-us-samad, the doctor of law, that I might employ myself in study and learning under the guidance of that illustrious teacher. Towards me he ever turned an eye of favour and kindness, and as his pupil I felt for him extreme affection and devotion, so that I passed four years in his service. When I first came there, I found two other pupils of mine own age newly arrived, Hakim Omar Khayyám, and the ill-fated Ben Sabbáh. Both were endowed with sharpness of wit and the highest natural powers; and we three formed a close friendship together. When the Imám rose from his lectures, they used to join me, and we repeated to each other the lessons we had heard. Now Omar was a native of Naishápúr, while Hasan Ben Sabbáh's father was one Ali, a man of austere Iife and practice, but heretical in his creed and doctrine. One day Hasan said to me and to Khayyám, 'It is a universal belief that the pupils of the Imám Mowaffak will attain to fortune. Now, even if we *all* do not attain thereto, without doubt one of us will; what then shall be our mutual pledge and bond?' We answered, 'Be it what you please.' 'Well,' he said, 'let us make a vow, that to whomsoever this fortune falls, he shall share it equally with the rest, and reserve no pre-eminence for himself.' 'Be it so,' we both replied, and on those terms we mutually pledged our words. Years rolled on, and I went from Khorassan to Transoxiana, and wandered to Ghazni and Cabul; and when I returned, I was invested with office, and rose to be administrator of affairs during the Sultanate of Sultan Alp Arslán.'

"He goes on to state, that years passed by, and both his old school-friends found him out, and came and claimed a share in his good fortune, according to the school-day vow. The Vizier was generous and kept his word. Hasan demanded a place in the government, which the Sultan granted at the Vizier's request; but discontented with a gradual rise, he plunged into the maze of intrigue of an oriental court, and, failing in a base attempt to supplant his benefactor, he was disgraced and fell. After many mishaps and wanderings, Hasan became the head of the Persian sect of the *Ismailians*,—a party of fanatics who had long murmured in obscurity, but rose to an evil eminence under the guidance of his strong and evil will. In A.D. 1090, he seized the castle of Alamút, in the province of Rúdbar, which lies in the mountainous tract south of the Caspian Sea; and it was from this mountain home he obtained that evil celebrity among the Crusaders as the OLD MAN OF THE MOUNTAINS, and spread terror through the Mohammedan world; and it is yet disputed whether the word *Assassin*, which they have left in the language of modern Europe as their dark memorial, is derived from the *hashish*, or opiate of hemp-leaves (the Indian *bhang*), with which they maddened themselves to the sullen pitch of oriental desperation, or from the name of the founder of the dynasty, whom we have seen in his quiet collegiate days, at Naishápúr. One of the countless victims of the Assassin's dagger was Nizám-ul-Mulk himself, the old school-boy friend.[1]

"Omar Khayyám also came to the Vizier to claim the share; but not to ask for title or office. 'The greatest boon you can confer on me,' he said, 'is to let me live in a corner under the shadow of your fortune, to spread wide the advantages of Science, and pray for your long life and prosperity.' The Vizier tells us, that, when he found Omar was really sincere in his refusal, he pressed him no further, but granted him a yearly pension of 1200 *mithkáls* of gold, from the treasury of Naishápúr.

"At Naishápúr thus lived and died Omar Khayyám, 'busied,' adds the Vizier, 'in winning knowledge of every kind, and especially in Astronomy, wherein he attained to a very high pre-eminence. Under the Sultanate of Malik Shah, he came to Merv, and obtained great praise for his proficiency in science, and the Sultan showered favours upon him.'

"When Malik Shah determined to reform the calendar, Omar was one of the eight learned men employed to do it; the result was the *Jaláli* era (so called from *Jalal-u-din*, one of the king's names)—'a computation of time,' says Gibbon, 'which surpasses the Julian, and approaches the accuracy of the Gregorian style.' He is also the author of some astronomical tables, entitled Zíji-Malikshíhí," and the French have lately republished and translated an Arabic Treatise of his on Algebra. *[In the first edition, this was followed by an extra section, which FitzGerald subsequently omitted.]*

"His Takhallus or poetical name (Khayyám) signifies a Tent-maker, and he is said to have at one time exercised that trade, perhaps before Nizám-ul-Mulk's generosity raised him to independence. Many Persian poets similarly derive their names from their occupations; thus we have Attár, 'a druggist,' Assár, 'an oil presser,' &c.[2] Omar himself alludes to his name in the following whimsical lines:—

'Khayyám, who stitched the tents of science,
Has fallen in grief's furnace and been suddenly burned;
The shears of Fate have cut the tent ropes of his life,
And the broker of Hope has sold him for nothing!'

"We have only one more anecdote to give of his Life, and that relates to the close; it is told in the anonymous preface which is sometimes prefixed to his poems; it has been printed in the Persian in the appendix to Hyde's *Veterum Persarum Religio*, p. 499; and D'Herbelot alludes to it in his Bibliothèque, under *Khiam*:[3]—

"'It is written in the chronicles of the ancients that this King of the Wise, Omar Khayyám, died at Naishápúr in the year of the Hegira, 517 (A.D. 1123); in science he was unrivalled,—the very paragon of his age. Khwájah Nizámi of Samarcand, who was one of his pupils, relates the following story: 'I often used to hold conversations with my teacher, Omar Khayyám, in a garden; and one day he said to me, 'My tomb shall be in a spot where the north wind may scatter roses over it.' I wondered at the words he spake, but I knew that his were no idle words.[4] Years after, when I chanced to revisit Naishápúr, I went to his final resting-place, and lo! it was just outside a garden, and trees laden with fruit stretched their boughs over the garden wall, and dropped their flowers upon his tomb, so as the stone was hidden under them.'"

Thus far—without fear of Trespass—from the *Calcutta Review*. The writer of it, on reading in India this story of Omar's Grave, was reminded he says, of Cicero's Account of finding Archimedes' Tomb at Syracuse, buried in grass and weeds. I think Thorwaldsen desired to have roses grow over him; a wish religiously fulfilled for him to the present day, I believe. However, to return to Omar.

Though the Sultan "shower'd Favours upon him," Omar's Epicurean Audacity of Thought and Speech caused him to be regarded askance in his own Time and Country. He is said to have been especially hated and dreaded by the Súfis, whose Practice he ridiculed, and whose Faith amounts to little more than his own when stript of the Mysticism and formal recognition of Islamism under which Omar would not hide. Their Poets, including Háfiz, who are (with the exception of Firdausi) the most considerable in Persia, borrowed largely, indeed, of Omar's material, but turning it to a mystical Use more convenient to Themselves and the People they addressed; a People quite as quick of Doubt as of Belief; as keen of Bodily Sense as of Intellectual; and delighting in a cloudy composition of both, in which they could float luxuriously between Heaven and Earth, and this World and the Next, on the wings of a poetical expression, that might serve indifferently for either. Omar was too honest of Heart as well as of Head for this. Having failed (however mistakenly) of finding any Providence but Destiny, and any World but This, he set about making the most of it; preferring rather to soothe the Soul through the Senses into Acquiescence with Things as he saw them, than to perplex it with vain disquietude after what they *might* be. It has been seen, however, that his Worldly Ambition was not exorbitant;

and he very likely takes a humorous or perverse pleasure in exalting the gratification of Sense above that of the Intellect, in which he must have taken great delight, although it failed to answer the Questions in which he, in common with all men, was most vitally interested. *[In the first edition, this was followed by an extra section, which FitzGerald subsequently omitted.]*

For whatever Reason, however, Omar, as before said, has never been popular in his own Country, and therefore has been but scantily transmitted abroad. The MSS. of his Poems, mutilated beyond the average Casualties of Oriental Transcription, are so rare in the East as scarce to have reacht Westward at all, in spite of all the acquisitions of Arms and Science. There is no copy at the India House, none at the Bibliothèque Nationale of Paris. We know but of one in England: No. 140 of the Ouseley MSS. at the Bodleian, written at Shiraz, A.D. 1460. This contains but 158 Rubáiyát. One in the Asiatic Society's Library at Calcutta (of which we have a Copy), contains (and yet incomplete) 516, though swelled to that by all kinds of Repetition and Corruption. So Von Hammer speaks of *his* Copy as containing about 200, while Dr. Sprenger catalogues the Lucknow MS. at double that number.[5] The Scribes, too, of the Oxford and Calcutta MSS. seem to do their Work under a sort of Protest; each beginning with a Tetrastich (whether genuine or not), taken out of its alphabetical order; the Oxford with one of Apology; the Calcutta with one of Expostulation, supposed (says a Notice prefixed to the MS.) to have risen from a Dream, in which Omar's mother asked about his future fate. It may be rendered thus:—

> "Oh Thou who burn'st in Heart for those who burn
> "In Hell, whose fires thyself shall feed in turn;
>   "How long be crying, 'Mercy on them, God!'
> "Why, who art Thou to teach, and He to learn?"

The Bodleian Quatrain pleads Pantheism by way of Justification.

> "If I myself upon a looser Creed
> "Have loosely strung the Jewel of Good deed,
> "Let this one thing for my Atonement plead:
> "That One for Two I never did mis-read."

The Reviewer, to whom I owe the Particulars of Omar's Life, concludes his Review by comparing him with Lucretius, both as to natural Temper and Genius, and as acted upon by the Circumstances in which he lived. Both indeed were men of subtle, strong, and cultivated Intellect, fine Imagination, and Hearts passionate for Truth and Justice; who justly revolted from their Country's false Religion, and false, or foolish, Devotion to it; but who fell short of replacing what they subverted by such better *Hope* as others, with no better Revelation to guide them, had yet made a Law to themselves. Lucretius, indeed, with such material as Epicurus furnished, satisfied himself with the theory of a vast machine fortuitously constructed, and acting by a Law that implied no Legislator; and so composing himself into a Stoical rather than Epicurean severity of Attitude, sat down to contemplate the mechanical Drama of the Universe which he was part Actor in; himself and all about him (as in his own sublime description of the Roman Theatre) discoloured with the lurid reflex of the Curtain suspended between the Spectator and the Sun. Omar, more desperate, or more careless of any so complicated System as resulted in nothing but hopeless Necessity, flung his own Genius and Learning with a bitter or humorous jest into the general Ruin which their insufficient glimpses only served to reveal; and, pretending sensual pleasure as the serious purpose of Life, only *diverted* himself with speculative problems of Deity, Destiny, Matter and Spirit, Good and Evil, and other such questions, easier to start than to run down, and the pursuit of which becomes a very weary sport at last!

With regard to the present Translation. The original Rubáiyát (as, missing an Arabic Guttural, these *Tetrastichs* are more musically called) are independent Stanzas, consisting each of four Lines of equal, though varied, Prosody; sometimes *all* rhyming, but oftener (as here imitated) the third line a blank. Something as in the Greek Alcaic, where the penultimate line seems to lift and suspend the Wave that falls over in the last. As usual with such kind of Oriental Verse, the Rubáiyát follow one another according to Alphabetic Rhyme—a strange succession of Grave and Gay. Those here selected are strung into something of an Eclogue, with perhaps a less than equal proportion of the "Drink and make-merry," which (genuine or not) recurs over-frequently in the Original. Either way, the Result is sad enough: saddest perhaps when most ostentatiously merry: more apt to move Sorrow than Anger toward the old Tentmaker, who, after vainly endeavouring to unshackle his Steps from Destiny, and to catch some authentic Glimpse of To-MORROW, fell back upon To-DAY (which has outlasted so many To-morrows!) as the only Ground he got to stand upon, however momentarily slipping from under his Feet.

[The following section and the accompanying notes were not included in the fourth edition. The text below is taken from FitzGerald's third edition; the bulk of it was initially published in the second edition.]

While the second Edition of this version of Omar was preparing, Monsieur Nicolas, French Consul at Resht, published a very careful and very good Edition of the Text, from a lithograph copy at Teheran, comprising 464 Rubáiyát, with translation and notes of his own.

Mons. Nicolas, whose Edition has reminded me of several things, and instructed me in others, does not consider Omar to be the material Epicurean that I have literally taken him for, but a Mystic, shadowing the Deity under the figure of Wine, Wine-bearer, &c., as Háfiz is supposed to do; in short, a Súfi Poet like Háfiz and the rest.

I cannot see reason to alter my opinion, formed as it was more than a dozen years ago when Omar was first shown me by one to whom I am indebted for all I know of Oriental, and very much of other, literature. He admired Omar's Genius so much, that he would gladly have adopted any such Interpretation of his meaning as Mons. Nicolas' if he could.[6] That he could not, appears by his Paper in the Calcutta Review already so largely quoted; in which he argues from the Poems themselves, as well as from what records remain of the Poet's Life.

And if more were needed to disprove his meaning as Mons. Nicolas', there is the Biographical Notice which he himself has drawn up in direct contradiction to the Interpretation of the Poems given in his Notes. (See pp. 13–14 of his Preface.) *[In the second edition, in place of this reference, FitzGerald quoted in French an extensive anecdote from Nicolas' Preface.]* Indeed I hardly knew poor Omar was so far gone till his Apologist informed me. For here we see that, whatever were the Wine that Háfiz drank and sang, the veritable Juice of the Grape it was which Omar used, not only when carousing with his friends, but (says Mons. Nicolas) in order to excite himself to that pitch of Devotion which others reached by cries and "hurlements *[yells]*." And yet, whenever Wine, Wine-bearer, &c., occur in the Text—which is often enough—Mons. Nicolas carefully annotates "Dieu, *[God]*" "La Divinité, *[Divinity]*" &c.: so carefully indeed that one is tempted to think that he was indoctrinated by the Súfi with whom he read the Poems. (Note to Rub. ii. p. 8.) A Persian would naturally wish to vindicate a distinguished Countryman; and a Súfi to enrol him in his own sect, which already comprises all the chief Poets of Persia.

What historical Authority has Mons. Nicolas to show that Omar gave himself up "avec passion à l'étude de la philosophie des Soufis *[with passion to the study of Súfi philosophy]*"? (Preface p. xiii.) The Doctrines of Pantheism, Materialism, Necessity, &c., were not peculiar to the Súfi; nor to Lucretius before them; nor to Epicurus before him; probably the very original Irreligion of Thinking men from the first; and very likely to be the spontaneous growth of a Philosopher living in an Age of social and political barbarism, under shadow of one of the Two and Seventy Religions supposed to divide the world. Von Hammer (according to Sprenger's Oriental Catalogue) speaks of Omar as "a Free-thinker, and *a great opponent of Sufism;*" perhaps because, while holding much of their Doctrine, he would not pretend to any inconsistent severity of morals. Sir W. Ouseley has written a Note to something of the same effect on the fly-leaf of the Bodleian MS. And in two Rubáiyát of Mons. Nicolas' own Edition Súf and Súfi are both disparagingly named.

No doubt many of these Quatrains seem unaccountable unless mystically interpreted; but many more as unaccountable unless literally. Were the Wine spiritual, for instance, how wash the Body with it when dead? Why make cups of the dead clay to be filled with—"La Divinité *[Divinity]*" by some succeeding Mystic? Mons. Nicolas himself is puzzled by some "bizarres *[bizarre]*",and "trop Orientales *[too Oriental]*" allusions and images—"d'une sensualité quelquefois révoltante *[of a sensuality that is sometimes revolting]*" indeed—-which "les covenances *[the proprieties]*" do not permit him to translate; but still which the reader cannot but refer to "La Divinité *[Divinity]*."[7] No doubt also many of the Quatrains in the Teheran, as in the Calcutta, Copies, are spurious; such *Rubáiyát* being the common form of Epigram in Persia. But this, at best, tells as much one way as another; nay, the Súfi, who may be considered the Scholar and Man of Letters in Persia, would be far more likely than the careless Epicure to interpolate what favours his own view of the Poet. I observe that very few of the more mystical Quatrains are in the Bodleian MS. which must be one of the oldest, as dated at Shiraz, A.H. 865, A.D. 1460. And this, I think, especially distinguishes Omar (I cannot help calling him by his—no, not Christian—familiar name) from all other Persian Poets: That, whereas with them the Poet is lost in his Song, the Man in Allegory and Abstraction; we seem to have the Man—the *Bonhomme* [*good fellow*]—Omar himself, with all his Humours and Passions, as frankly before us as if we were really at Table with him, after the Wine had gone round.

I must say that I, for one, never wholly believed in the Mysticism of Háfiz. It does not appear there was any danger in holding and singing Súfi Pantheism, so long as the Poet made his Salaam to Mohammed at the beginning and end of his Song. Under such conditions Jeláluddín, Jámi, Attár, and others sang; using Wine and Beauty indeed as Images to illustrate, not as a Mask to hide, the Divinity they were celebrating. Perhaps some Allegory less liable to mistake or abuse had been better among so inflammable a People: much more so when, as some think with Háfiz and Omar, the abstract is not only likened to, but identified with, the sensual Image; hazardous, if not to the Devotee himself, yet to his weaker Brethren; and worse for the Profane in proportion as the Devotion of the Initiated grew warmer. And all for what? To be tantalized with Images of sensual enjoyment which must be renounced if one would approximate a God, who according to the Doctrine, *is* Sensual Matter as well as Spirit, and into whose Universe one expects unconsciously to merge after Death, without hope of any posthumous Beatitude in another world to compensate for all one's self-denial in this. Lucretius' blind Divinity certainly merited, and probably got, as much self-sacrifice as this of the Súfi; and the burden of Omar's Song—if not "Let us eat"—is assuredly—"Let us drink, for Tomorrow we die!" And if Háfiz meant quite otherwise by a similar language, he surely miscalculated when he devoted his Life and Genius to so equivocal a Psalmody as, from his Day to this, has been said and sung by any rather than spiritual Worshippers.

However, as there is some traditional presumption, and certainly the opinion of some learned men, in favour of Omar's being a Súfi—and even something of a Saint—those who please may so interpret his Wine and Cup-bearer. On the other hand, as there is far more historical certainty of his being a Philosopher, of scientific Insight and Ability far beyond that of the Age and Country he lived in; of such moderate worldly Ambition as becomes a Philosopher, and such moderate wants as rarely satisfy a Debauchee; other readers may be content to believe with me that, while the Wine Omar celebrates is simply the Juice of the Grape, he bragg'd more than he drank of it, in very Defiance perhaps of that Spiritual Wine which left its Votaries sunk in Hypocrisy or Disgust.

Notes to the Preface

[1] Some of Omar's Rubáiyát warn us of the danger of Greatness, the instability of Fortune, and while advocating Charity to all Men, recommending us to be too intimate with none. Attár makes Nizám-ul-Mulk use the very words of his friend Omar [Rub. xxviii.], "When Nizám-ul-Mulk was in the Agony (of Death) he said, 'Oh God! I am passing away in the hand of the Wind.'" *[Reference is to quatrain 28 in both first and fourth editions.]*

[2] Though all these, like our Smiths, Archers, Millers, Fletchers, &c., may simply retain the Surname of an hereditary calling.

[3] "Philosophe Musulman qui a vécu en Odeur de Sainteté dans sa Religion, vers la Fin du premier et le Commencement du second Siècle de l'Hegire, *[Muslim philosopher who lived in the good graces of his religion, towards the end of the first and beginning of the second century of the Hejira]*" no part of which, except the "Philosophe, *[philosopher]*" can apply to *our* Khayyám.

[4] The Rashness of the Words, according to D'Herbelot, consisted in being so opposed to those in the Korán: "No Man knows where he shall die."—This Story of Omar reminds me of another so naturally—and, when one remembers how wide of his humble mark the noble sailor aimed—so pathetically told by Captain Cook—not by Doctor Hawkesworth—in his Second Voyage. When leaving Ulietea, "Oreo's last request was for me to return. When he saw he could not obtain that promise, he asked the name of my *Marai*—Burying-place. As strange a question as this was, I hesitated not a moment to tell him 'Stepney,' the parish in which I live when in London. I was made to repeat it several times over till they could pronounce it; and then 'Stepney Marai no Toote' was echoed through an hundred mouths at once. I afterwards found the same question had been put to Mr. Forster by a man on shore; but he gave a different, and indeed more proper answer, by saying, 'No man who used the sea could say where he should be buried.'"

[5] "Since this Paper was written" (adds the Reviewer in a note), "we have met with a Copy of a very rare Edition, printed at Calcutta in 1836. This contains 438 Tetrastichs, with an Appendix containing 54 others not found in some MSS."

[6] Perhaps would have edited the Poems himself some years ago. He may now as little approve of my Version on one side, as of Mons. Nicolas' Theory on the other.

[7] A note to Quatrain 234 admits that, however clear the mystical meaning of such Images must be to Europeans, they are not quoted without "rougissant [*blushing*]" even by laymen in Persia—"Quant aux termes de tendresse qui commencent ce quatrain, comme tant d'autres dans ce recueil, nos lecteurs, habitués maintenant à l'étrangeté des expressions si souvent employées par Khèyam pour rendre ses pensées sur l'amour divin, et à la singularité des images trop orientales, d'une sensualité quelquefois révoltante, n'auront pas de peine à se persuader qu'il s'agit de la Divinité, bien que cette conviction soit vivement discutée par les moullahs musulmans, et même par beaucoup de laïques, qui rougissent véritablement d'une pareille licence de leur compatriote à l'égard des choses spirituelles. *[As for the terms of endearment that start this quatrain, like many others in this collection, our readers, now used to the strangeness of the expressions so often used by Khayyám to present his thoughts on divine love, and to the peculiarity of images too oriental, of a sensuality that is sometimes revolting, will not have difficulty in persuading themselves that it has to do with the Divinity, even though this conviction is keenly discussed by muslim mullahs, and even by many lay people, who truly blush at such licence being taken by their compatriot with regard to spiritual matters.]*"

Figure 2 Two images of Omar Khayyám – in Nishápúr and Samarkand.

آمد که آنکه خیمکها اندر دوش

گویند که پشت پشت حمال آمد

تمّت الرّباعیات

کتبه العبد المفتقر الی رحمة الملك الباقی
شیخ محمود یربوداقی فی العشر الاخر من
صفر ختم بالخیر والظفر بسنه خمس وستّین و
ثمانمائه الهجریّه النبویّه علیه السّلم والتّحیّة
والاکرام بدار الملك شیراز .

حماها الله تعالی عن الاعواز

Figure 3 The final page of the Ouseley manuscript of the *Rubáiyát* with Edward
Heron-Allen's transcription of the Persian text.

Figure 4 Elihu Vedder's illustration for quatrain 90 in the third edition of the *Rubáiyát* (1884).

Figure 5 Cover of 'gift book' copy of the *Rubáiyát* illustrated by René Bull (1913).

Figure 6 Ronald Balfour's illustration for quatrain 9 in the first edition of the *Rubáiyát* (1920).

Figure 7 Cover of first known musical setting of the *Rubáiyát*, by Liza Lehmann in 1896.

Figure 8 Omar Khayyám used as a brand name for wine in Egypt and India.

Figure 9 A modern interpretation of quatrain 11 of the first edition, by Suzanne Jones, 2009.

Part 2

The *Rubáiyát*,
Its Story and Its Influence

Omar Khayyám and His *Rubáiyát*

The Historical Omar Khayyám

The story of the *Rubáiyát of Omar Khayyám* involves two authors, the Persian Omar Khayyám and the Englishman Edward FitzGerald. It begins in mediaeval Persia, in the province of Khorasan in the northeast of what is modern day Iran. The historical Omar Khayyám was born in 1048 in the prosperous city of Nishápúr (Figure 2). He died in the same place round about 1131, having travelled widely over his eighty odd years, living and working also in the great cities of Samarkand, Bokhara, Merv and Isfahán, and making the long journey to Mecca.[1]

Although people in the West associate the name Omar Khayyám with poetry, the historical Khayyám was an astronomer, mathematician and philosopher. Little is known definitively about Khayyám's life, though recently Hazhir Teimourian produced an illuminating 'biography' using such data as are available from a very ill documented period.[2] The story of the friendship between the astronomer-poet Khayyám, the Seljuk vizier Nizám al Mulk and the assassin Hasan Sabbáh, recounted by FitzGerald in his preface (see page 71), is now known to be untrue.[3] But, it is clear that Khayyám lived and worked for an important part of his time at the court of the Seljuk rulers, and his thinking and writing were carried out in, and shaped by, what was a difficult political and religious environment.[4]

Politically, in Khayyám's time, the region of Iran was divided into a series of princedoms, whose leaders, although nominally owing allegiance to the Islamic Caliph in Baghdad, were very much absolute rulers in their own territories. Power changed from time to time as new warlords emerged from the Turkic lands to the East, from what is now known as Turkmenistan and beyond. This process of invasion from the East culminated, nearly 100 years after Khayyám's death, in the crushing wave of power unleashed by Genghis Khan and his Mongol 'hordes', who arrived in eastern Iran in the early part of the thirteenth century.

Religion was also an important element shaping the society and the power structure of this early period. Iran had been a Muslim country since the Arab armies had spread Islam outwards from the Arabian peninsula in the seventh century CE. But, up to around the time of Khayyám's birth in the middle eleventh century, there had been fairly open discussion about the precise nature of Islamic thinking and beliefs, and the legal system or *sharia* which was based on them. For at least two centuries, Islamic philosophers and theologians had a good deal of freedom to explore fundamental questions about God and the origins and purpose of the world, and to investigate the views of earlier writers and thinkers, including famous Greek philosophers like Plato and Aristotle. But in the eleventh century, this freedom of thought began to be curtailed, as Islamic beliefs came to be codified and enforced more precisely. For prominent people, particularly those at court, it started to be dangerous to express opinions that did not concur with the accepted views.

As we shall see below, this change in religious and philosophical freedom is important to the understanding of both the content and the history of the *Rubáiyát* of Omar Khayyám. Meanwhile, it is worth noting that, in his professional scientific fields, Khayyám left important writings and legacies; these have been extensively reviewed in the West, most recently by Mehdi Aminrazavi in his book *The Wine of Wisdom*.[5] As an astronomer, Khayyám helped with a major reorganisation of the Persian calendar, based on calculations of the movement of the stars that retained their validity until well into the twentieth century. He was involved with the creation of a major new observatory in Isfahán, which alas no longer exists. In the field of mathematics, Khayyám is known for providing the solution to a key algebraic problem, while he also left a number of more technical writings on the interpretation of Islamic law.

Omar Khayyám the Poet

The reputation of the historical Omar Khayyám as a scientist is well established, in the West as well as the East. But his position as a poet is more uncertain. Indeed, there is some doubt as to whether the historical Khayyám actually composed any poetry at all.

Because of the continual invasions and wars in eastern Iran in the mediaeval period, there are few surviving documents from the eleventh and twelfth centuries, the period in which Khayyám lived. The writings that we know of from the period exist mainly as later copies of works that it is believed were created in that time. Certainly there is no evidence showing that any verses by Khayyám were written down during his lifetime. The material that exists suggests, if anything, the reverse. In a famous twelfth century review, the author Nizámi Aruzi does not mention Omar Khayyám in his section on poets, though he refers to Khayyám as a scientist. Nizámi knew Khayyám personally, meeting him when the author was a child and the scientist was an old man. He quotes the story of how he visited Khayyám's grave some years after the famous man's death, and found it covered by two kinds of fruit blossom, exactly as Khayyám himself had predicted.[6]

Some verses began to be attributed to Khayyám around 50 years after his death. In the 1170s, an anthology of Khorasan poets writing in Arabic contains four verses by Omar Khayyám. In the following (thirteenth) century other writers began to refer to Persian verses attributed to an author of this name. Over the subsequent centuries the number of Persian verses included in manuscript collections under the name of Khayyám grew, and complete manuscripts of 'his' poetry began to be produced. One of the most famous of the latter is the so-called Ouseley manuscript, now in the Bodleian Library in Oxford, which was Edward FitzGerald's first introduction to the *Rubáiyát* of Omar Khayyám. This manuscript is dated 1460–61, and it contains a total of 158 verses. Later collections added further verses to the total attributed to Khayyám; the largest of these, dated 1893, is reported to have over 1,000 verses.

At the end of the nineteenth century, scholars of Persian literature in the West began to question the attribution of so many verses to the name of Omar Khayyám. Detailed analyses, by academics and others from Russia, Germany, the UK and elsewhere, identified verses that appear also in the collections of other poets' work and can more correctly be attributed to them. These so-called 'wandering' verses numbered several hundreds, and scholars have also discounted other verses in the Khayyám collections as being unlikely to be from the same hand, owing to their very different style and content.[7]

The result of this work is that, according to current expert opinion, less than 200 of the verses at one time attributed to Omar Khayyám can reasonably be considered to be by this poet.[8] But there are further questions, perhaps even more important, raised by the modern research. Was the poet, who wrote the verses now collected together, actually the same person as the historical Omar Khayyám, the famous scientist, mathematician and philosopher? Were there two Omar Khayyáms, one a scientist and the other a poet? And were the poems, even the reduced number of under 200, all written by the same hand, or should one rather talk about a number of poets who wrote verses with similar content, sentiment and style, a kind of Khayyámic school of poets?

Much has been written on these questions and those interested are referred especially to the work of Aminrazavi mentioned above, and François de Blois' masterly review of Persian literature of the mediaeval period.[9] As editors, we take the view that these questions, while fascinating, are probably impossible to answer, and do not, in any event, have an important bearing on the story of FitzGerald's *Rubáiyát of Omar Khayyám*, which is our prime concern. However, we shall return to them, and to the vital question of 'Khayyám's' religious and philosophical position as expressed in the verses, when we discuss the *Rubáiyát* itself in more detail (page 109).

The Discovery of Khayyám in the West

The name of Omar Khayyám first became known in the West in the sixteenth century through his astronomical work. His work on the calendar was mentioned by the German scientist Joseph Scaliger in 1583. A manuscript of Khayyam's algebraic calculations was acquired fairly early by Leiden University in the Netherlands, and it has been suggested that it could have influenced the work of René Descartes in this field in the seventeenth century.[10]

Verses under the name Omar Khayyám were first recognised at the beginning of the eighteenth century when one was translated (into Latin) by Thomas Hyde in his work on the Religions of the Ancient Persians. Various orientalists, who travelled in the Middle East and India in subsequent years, collected manuscripts of Persian poetry, including William Ouseley who somewhere acquired the manuscript of the *Rubáiyát* that now bears his name. But it was not until over a century after Thomas Hyde, in 1818, that an Austrian scholar Joseph von Hammer included 25 verses from Omar Khayyám in a collection of Persian verses translated into German. This translation was used by Louisa Stuart Costello as the basis for an English version, first published in Fraser's Magazine in 1840.[11]

There were thus only a very few other translations available before 1856 when Khayyám's *Rubáiyát* was brought to the attention of Edward FitzGerald. The story of how this happened continues below.

Edward FitzGerald and His *Rubáiyát*

FitzGerald's Origins and Upbringing

Edward FitzGerald will always be best known as the creator of a poem called the *Rubáiyát of Omar Khayyám*. But he was actually a much more interesting and complex man than this simple description implies. Furthermore, the nature of, and background to, FitzGerald's life had an important influence on his interpretation of the *Rubáiyát*, and this can tell us something about the quality and success of the verses he created.[12]

FitzGerald is best described as a well-to-do Victorian man of letters. He was born in 1809 in Bredfield near Woodbridge in Suffolk. For the whole of his life of 74 years he was based mainly in East Anglia, though he travelled extensively round the UK and even visited the continent several times. He died in Merton in Norfolk in 1883.

The FitzGerald family were very well-off landowners of Irish descent. Edward's father's name was originally John Purcell. His mother, Mary FitzGerald, inherited extensive properties from her own family, and this led to the Purcell family changing their name to FitzGerald. Mrs. FitzGerald became, reputedly, the wealthiest woman in England. Edward FitzGerald's upbringing was perhaps typical of a wealthy Victorian family. He was the sixth of eight children, with five sisters and two brothers. His parents were rather distant figures who did not spend much time with their children. FitzGerald later describes how 'My Mother used to come up sometimes [*to the nursery*], and we Children were not much comforted.'[13] With the exception of his sister Eleanor, who was four years older, he was not close to his siblings, but he remained in touch with his family throughout his life.

The family moved house several times in FitzGerald's youth, including two years living in France, in and around Paris. In 1818, at age nine, Edward was sent, with his older brothers, as a boarder to King Edward VI Grammar School in Bury St. Edmunds, where he stayed until 1826 when he was admitted to Trinity College, Cambridge.

At both school and university, FitzGerald made close friends, whom he was to keep as such throughout his life.

The Importance of Friendship

Friendship is a key theme in the life of Edward FitzGerald. As a man of independent means, who did not need to work for pay, he devoted much of his time in adulthood to his many friends, writing to them frequently, visiting them often for quite long periods, and joining them for cultural activities such as visits to concerts, art galleries and theatres, particularly in London. Fortunately, a large number (over 1000) of his letters have been preserved and published in four collected volumes, which give a detailed picture of his life and social networks, and the interests, intellectual and other, which occupied his daily life and thought. He was intensely loyal to his friends, who sometimes did not respond as often or as quickly to his letters as he might have wished. As a rather shy, sometimes eccentric character, he was easily put off by social contacts (Figure 1). But he had a wide acquaintance and he maintained an active social life even in his later years.[14]

Many of his friendships reflect his intellectual and literary pursuits. Among his literary friends were three of the great Victorian writers, William Makepeace Thackeray (the novelist), Alfred Lord Tennyson (the poet laureate), and Thomas Carlyle (the historian and essayist). Thackeray and Tennyson were contemporaries of FitzGerald at Cambridge, though he did not actually meet Tennyson until some years after coming down from university. FitzGerald met and corresponded with these two frequently, and also provided them with financial help in their early years. Both acknowledged the value of his friendship; Tennyson included a poem 'To E. FitzGerald' in his collection *Tiresias and other poems*, published after his friend's death.[15] FitzGerald was introduced to Thomas Carlyle in 1842. At that time, the historian was working on his biography of Oliver Cromwell, and FitzGerald did some research for him on the battlefield of Naseby, the site of which lay within the FitzGerald family's properties.

Almost all of FitzGerald's close friendships were with men, though he always stayed in contact with his sister Eleanor and her family, and, in later life, he maintained a regular correspondence with Fanny Kemble, the actress sister of his old school friend John Kemble.[16]

Many of his friends and correspondents were men of his own age, but he also developed close relationships with a number of younger men who often did not share fully his intellectual and literary interests. One was William Browne, an active young landowner in Bedfordshire, in whose house FitzGerald stayed when he was working on the *Rubáiyát*. Browne was tragically killed by a riding accident in 1859, just as the *Rubáiyát* was published.

A key friendship in FitzGerald's later years was that with Joseph 'Posh' Fletcher, an uneducated fisherman with whom FitzGerald went into partnership in a commercial fishing venture. It has been suggested that FitzGerald's involvement with these younger men implies that he was homosexual in orientation.[17] There is no definitive evidence on this, though undoubtedly his brief marriage to Lucy Barton, mentioned below, was a disaster. This question has some relevance to the interpretation of FitzGerald's *Rubáiyát*, an issue to which we shall return in due course.

An Early Interest in Language

In his early adult life, Edward FitzGerald spent much time acting as escort to his mother, particularly in London society. He also kept in touch with his friends and enjoyed evenings of convivial discussion. His letters show that he occupied himself with the intellectual issues of the day and gradually with other writings of his own.[18] His first poem, entitled 'The Meadows in Spring', was published in 1831; it is a eulogy of the Suffolk countryside to which FitzGerald remained devoted throughout his life. His first complete book, *Euphranor: A Dialogue on Youth*, was published in 1851. This deals with the author's concern about the state of British education at the time, and is in the form of a discussion taking place in Cambridge between four students and an older physician; the setting and content highlight the importance of FitzGerald's university years in his personal development. *Euphranor* also set another precedent in that, like most of his later works, particularly the first edition of the *Rubáiyát*, FitzGerald organised and paid for the printing and distribution of the book himself.

FitzGerald always had an interest in languages, including the dialects of his own region. As a schoolboy and young man, he had made many translations from the classics, and a number of his friends from that period shared this interest. But it was a meeting with a much younger man, Edward Cowell, which took FitzGerald into the area of serious translation, and which led on to the creation of the *Rubáiyát*.

At the time of their meeting in 1844, Cowell was aged 18 and FitzGerald 35 years. Cowell was an exceptional linguist who later, after spending some years in India, became Professor of Sanskrit at Cambridge University. By the age of 16, Cowell had mastered Latin, Greek, Spanish and Persian, and started on Sanskrit, which he '... found too hard...' to start with.[19] After several meetings, Cowell introduced his new friend to Spanish, which FitzGerald took up with enthusiasm. By the early 1850's the latter had become proficient enough to translate and publish English versions of six plays by a famous Spanish writer, Calderón. Once again FitzGerald organised and paid for the publication himself.

Cowell had begun to study the Persian language in 1841 at the age of 15 years, and he made some translations from Háfiz and other poets which he showed to FitzGerald. When the latter was visiting Cowell and his wife in Oxford late in 1852, Cowell suggested to his friend that he should take up Persian, and he sent FitzGerald a copy of Sir William Jones' *Grammar of the Persian Language* on which to base his studies. The idea clearly appealed to FitzGerald, who spent nearly a year immersed in the language. Later on in his Persian studies, he wrote to Cowell: 'As to Jones' Grammar, I have a sort of *love* for it!'[20] He then went on to try his hand at translating some of the Persian poets, working especially on Háfiz, Jámi and Attár. In 1856, he published an English version of Jámi's *Salámán and Ábsál*. This was, as he put it, a 'little monument' to his first Persian work with Edward Cowell.[21]

Creating the *Rubáiyát*

It is a happy coincidence that FitzGerald was already well prepared for translation from the Persian by the time Omar Khayyám came into his life. The story is one that has been told often.[22] In 1856, while working as an assistant in the Bodleian Library in Oxford, Cowell discovered a manuscript of *Rubáiyát* attributed to Omar Khayyám. This was what is known as the Ouseley manuscript, mentioned on page 95 (Figure 3). Cowell made a copy of the manuscript in a small notebook and sent it to FitzGerald. This copy, with FitzGerald's notes on it, is now in the University Library in Cambridge.

FitzGerald was captivated by the verses from eleventh-century Persia. He appears to have been stimulated both by Khayyám's poetry and its content. He worked on and off for two years on his interpretation or 'rendering' of the *Rubáiyát* into English. In May 1857, he sent the author George Borrow a quatrain by 'one Omar Khayyám who was an Epicurean Infidel some 500 years ago...' He later told Cowell about his affinity for the Persian poet, suggesting that Cowell could not 'feel *with* him [*Khayyám*] in some respects as I do.'[23]

The method that FitzGerald adopted in creating his *Rubáiyát of Omar Khayyám* is of interest. According to later comments by Edward Cowell, FitzGerald used to read a few Persian verses and make a translation of them which he retained in his memory. He would then go for a walk and only on his return would he create an interpretation of them; some of his first efforts at such 'translation' were made into Latin, and only later on did he change to producing English verse. The English version was intended as a free interpretation, sometimes combining more than one Persian verse; we return to this aspect of the *Rubáiyát* on page 106 below. FitzGerald himself commented on the free quality of his 'translation': 'Better a live Sparrow than a stuffed Eagle.'[24]

Work on the *Rubáiyát* helped FitzGerald through a difficult passage in his own life, brought on by the departure of Cowell and his wife (both close friends) to India in 1856, and his own unfortunate (and short lived) marriage to Lucy Barton later in the same year. Lucy was the daughter of his old friend Bernard Barton (the Quaker poet), who had died in 1849, and FitzGerald appears to have felt himself committed to her by a promise made to her father before he died. The story of the relationship is both complex and sad.[25] The marriage did not take place until seven years after Barton's death and it was only a few months before the couple separated. FitzGerald worked on the *Rubáiyát* during the summer after the marriage, writing to Cowell that 'Omar breaths a sort of Consolation to me!'[26]

Meanwhile, in autumn 1856, Cowell, now in Calcutta, found another Khayyám manuscript; he had that copied and sent it to FitzGerald. The latter worked on both manuscripts through 1857, producing an initial set of 35 English verses which he sent for publication to *Fraser's Magazine* early in 1858. When, later in the year, he had heard nothing from the editor of *Fraser's*, he withdrew those verses. Early in 1859, having added a further 40 verses, making a total of 75, FitzGerald had

250 copies of these printed at his own expense. The little pamphlet, in a plain brown paper wrapper, had on its title page: *Rubáiyát of Omar Khayyám, The Astronomer-Poet of Persia: Translated into English Verse*. There was no attribution to FitzGerald as author or translator. He retained 40 copies to give to friends, and left the remainder with Bernard Quaritch the bookseller, to sell on his behalf. The book was advertised for sale by Quaritch in March 1859 at one shilling. In this way, a great poem crept quietly into the public view.[27]

A Work Continually in Progress

The fascinating history of the *Rubáiyát* in publication is continued on page 111. But there is more to tell about FitzGerald's involvement with the poem.[28] After publishing his first edition in 1859, FitzGerald paid little attention to the work for several years. He set up residence in Woodbridge, took up sailing in quite a big way, and moved on to work on other topics, including East Anglian dialects and more translations from Spanish and the classics. But, in 1867, he obtained a copy of a French prose translation of the *Rubáiyát* by J. B. Nicolas.[29] This revived FitzGerald's interest in his *Rubáiyát*, at a time when Quaritch was asking for permission to produce a new edition of the book which was beginning to attract public attention. FitzGerald revised the wording of some of his first set of verses, removed two and added a further 37 new quatrains, a few of them based on Nicolas' work. These 110 verses were published as the second edition of the *Rubáiyát* in 1868, now described as being 'Rendered into English verse'. The print run was only 200 copies, slightly less than for the first edition, and there was again no attribution of the English poem to FitzGerald. Indeed, no version of it with his name attached was published during the poet's lifetime.

FitzGerald continued to revise his *Rubáiyát* during subsequent years, producing two other authorised versions; a fifth version, with further minor changes found in FitzGerald's papers, was published after his death, initially as part of the first edition of his *Letters and Literary Remains*, which came out in 1889.[30] The third, fourth and fifth editions all comprise 101 verses, and they are virtually identical except in punctuation. As can be seen in Part 1, the wording of some of the verses was revised from the second edition, and nine verses were discarded. In his later years, FitzGerald turned his attention as a writer more to the classics, though he also finished a version of the Persian mystical work by Attár, *The Conference of the Birds*. He insisted that his earlier version of Jámi's *Salámán and Ábsál* should be included with the *Rubáiyát* in the fourth edition of the latter; the print run of this 1879 edition was sharply increased to 1000 copies at the insistence of Bernard Quaritch, who was again the publisher.

The poet remained based in Woodbridge for the rest of his life and was considered somewhat eccentric by the local residents; he was apparently nicknamed 'Dotty' by local wits.[31] His letters show that he maintained his intellectual interests despite failing eyesight, and he kept in continual contact with many of his friends, with occasional visits to London and elsewhere. Alfred Tennyson and his son visited him in Woodbridge in 1876. FitzGerald died in May 1883 while on a visit to his friend Crabbe (grandson of the poet George Crabbe) in Merton in Norfolk. He is buried in the churchyard at Boulge, a village near Woodbridge in Suffolk, not far from Bredfield, where he was born.

The Poem Itself

What is a Rubáiyát?

As indicated in the Introduction to Part 1 (page viii), the word *'rubáiyát'* is related to the Arabic word *'arba'a'* which means 'four'. A *'rubái'* is a four-line verse, and *'rubáiyát'* is the plural of this word, thus meaning a collection of four-line verses. The equivalent Latin based word for a four-line verse is a 'quatrain', so the *Rubáiyát* is a collection of quatrains.

There is much more that can be said about the tradition of the *rubáiyát* in Persian poetry. Readers with a particular interest in this are referred especially to works by Peter Avery and J. T. P. de Bruijn.[32] From the point of view of understanding Khayyám's verses and FitzGerald's *Rubáiyát*, the following are important points.

First, while the *rubáiyát* is a long established form of Persian poetry, it is not considered to be a particularly important type of poetical writing. It is something that a poet, or an educated literary person, might toss off in a spare moment, or compose when spending a convivial evening with friends. The verses can be likened to the western epigram or the Japanese *haiku*, and Avery suggests that they were sometimes used to express political or social dissent. Even today, Persian literary analysts do not rate writers of *rubáiyát* highly, which explains perhaps why the verses of Khayyám were not widely recognised as important in Iran until FitzGerald's interpretation of them began to penetrate from the West. We return to this point on page 120 below.

Second, in the Persian tradition, a *rubáiyát* is simply a collection of individual verses. There is no story line or continuity between the quatrains, and they are usually presented in Persian in alphabetical order of the final rhymes. As we shall see, FitzGerald made a radical innovation in this respect in his *Rubáiyát*. Third, in Persian, there is a distinctive rhythm and rhyming scheme for the verses in a *rubáiyát*; generally the latter is AABA. The following verse shows that FitzGerald followed the Persian tradition in his rhyming scheme, but he chose a more conventional English rhythm or metre for his verses.[33]

> Dreaming when Dawn's Left Hand was in the **Sky**
> I heard a Voice within the Tavern **cry**,
>   "Awake, my Little ones, and fill the Cup
> "Before Life's Liquor in its Cup be **dry**." F1:Q2
> *[editors' emboldening]*[34]

How FitzGerald Used His Sources

We outlined above how FitzGerald based his versions of the *Rubáiyát of Omar Khayyám* on a selection of the verses in two manuscripts given to him by Cowell. These were the Ouseley manuscript of 1460–61 and the longer Calcutta manuscript of an unknown but probably later date. In modern terminology, the Victorian poet 'cherry picked' from the Persian originals, selecting the quatrains that appealed to him to include as the basis for the total of less than 120 different verses which were included in the three main versions of his *Rubáiyát*. FitzGerald's original manuscript sources have a total of more than 600 quatrains (including overlaps), to which must be added some additional verses contained in the sources used by Nicolas for his French translation, which FitzGerald used in preparing his second edition.

It is helpful to look more closely at the links between the Persian material and FitzGerald's English verse. The late Victorian scholar and polymath Edward Heron-Allen made a comprehensive analysis of the Persian sources for each of FitzGerald's quatrains, identifying which of the Khayyám quatrains in his view fitted best with the English version. We show below two examples taken from this work, first published in 1899. Heron-Allen's analysis was reviewed, with some corrections, by Arberry in 1959.[35]

Our first example is the very first quatrain of the first edition, where FitzGerald's prime source has been identified as quatrain 134 from the Calcutta manuscript. Heron-Allen's fairly literal translation of these four lines is:

> The Sun casts the noose of morning upon the roofs,
> Kai Khosru of the day, he throws a stone into the bowl:
> Drink wine! For the Herald of the Dawn, rising up,
> Hurls into the days the cry of "Drink ye!" (Calcutta MS:Q134)

FitzGerald turned the underlying sentiment of this verse into the following English poetry:

AWAKE! for Morning in the Bowl of Night
Has flung the Stone that puts the Stars to Flight:
　　And Lo! the Hunter of the East has caught
The Sultán's Turret in a Noose of Light. (F1:Q1)

A second example is the famous quatrain number 11 from the first edition, which became number 12 in the later editions, with some significant changes in wording. FitzGerald's first version of this quatrain runs as follows:

Here with a Loaf of Bread beneath the Bough,
A Flask of Wine, a Book of Verse—and Thou
　　Beside me singing in the Wilderness—
And Wilderness is Paradise enow. (F1:Q11)

Heron-Allen suggests that FitzGerald derived this verse by combining sentiments from two quatrains, both in the Ouseley manuscript (one of which is also in the Calcutta original). Again, in a literal translation by Heron-Allen, these verses run:

If a loaf of wheaten bread be forthcoming,
A gourd of wine, and a thigh-bone of mutton,
And then, if thou and I be sitting in the wilderness, -
That were a joy not within the power of any Sultan.
　　　　　(Ouseley MS:Q135; Calcutta MS:Q474)

I desire a flask of ruby wine and a book of verses
Just enough to keep me alive, and half a loaf is needful,
And then, that thou and I should sit in the wilderness,
Is better than the kingdom of a Sultan. (Ouseley MS Q149)

Even a cursory examination of these texts shows that FitzGerald's interpretation of the original is very free, and we have already noted that the poet saw his writing not as a translation but as an attempt to render the Persian verse and thought into a good English poem. Over the 150 years of the existence of FitzGerald's *Rubáiyát*, there have been a number of Persian specialists who have criticised this aspect of his work.[36] But even his critics have generally agreed that he succeeded both in creating great verse and in getting into the spirit of the Persian original. A Persian writer has said that 'FitzGerald's poem is an independent masterpiece inspired by the spirit of Khayyám'. More recently, a western expert in Persian literature has spoken of 'the memorable intensity' of the *Rubáiyát*, which, as he continues, 'undoubtedly comes from FitzGerald's sense that he had found a twin soul in Khayyám'.[37]

The Structure and Content of the Poem

As well as taking considerable liberties with the language and content of individual verses, FitzGerald also abandoned the Persian tradition of each quatrain being a stand alone sentiment, with no specific links to others in the collection. He turned the sentiments expressed in the original verses into a more coherent sequence. The story line of FitzGerald's *Rubáiyát* flows from the light of dawn and youth, through the ups and downs and philosophical concerns of mid-day and middle age, to thoughts of evening and death. In fact it can be seen not just as a day in the life of the poet, as FitzGerald suggested, but also as the feelings of an older man looking back on his life and forward to his imminent death.[38] In the first edition it is Khayyám the poet who takes the reader on his journey or invites him to stay awhile: 'oh come with old Khayyám, and leave the Lot...' (F1:Q9). Interestingly, in his later editions, FitzGerald removed the references to Khayyám by name, except in the title of the poem, though he retained the sense of a poet as narrator.[39]

Another feature of FitzGerald's re-ordering of the Persian quatrains was the collection together of a number of verses about pots and their concerns in a special section. In the first edition this was called the *Kúza-Náma* or Book of the Pots, though this title was removed in FitzGerald's later versions. Here, through seven verses (increased to nine after the first edition), the narrator visits the potter's shop and observes the pots' conversations and complaints, which '...Some could articulate, while others not...' (F1:Q60) They provide some of the most telling imagery in the *Rubáiyát*, as when, for example, 'A Vessel of more ungainly Make' comments '"They sneer at me for leaning all awry / What! did the Hand then of the Potter shake?'" (F1:Q63)

Both Khayyám and FitzGerald were concerned with the uncertainties of life – what is the basic purpose of human existence and what happens to us after death? Like their Persian originals, the English verses do not provide answers to these questions. It is not for nothing that the *Rubáiyát* has been called the agnostic's bible. As FitzGerald puts it,

> 'Tis all a Chequer-board of Nights and Days
> Where Destiny with Men for Pieces plays:
> Hither and thither moves, and mates, and slays,
> And one by one back in the Closet lays. (F1:Q49)

Not all verses of the *Rubáiyát* have a meaning that is entirely clear and much time and energy has been devoted to analysing and interpreting the *Rubáiyát*, both from the original Persian sources, and in FitzGerald's versions. For example, Persian scholars have been concerned to establish whether or not 'Khayyám', either the historical figure or another more shadowy entity, was at heart a believer in Islam, and also whether he can be regarded as following the more mystical Súfi tradition in the Islamic faith. The evidence on both these questions appears to be very ambiguous. FitzGerald's introductions provide some comments on the subject (see page 77), and readers interested in these questions are also referred to Aminrazavi's book for one of the most recent summaries of the issues.[40]

A Source of Religious and Social Controversy

It may well be the acceptance of uncertainty and the lack of dogmatic belief evident in the Persian verses that drew FitzGerald to the *Rubáiyát* of Omar Khayyám. FitzGerald, while remaining a member of the Church of England, had considerable doubts about the nature of Anglican beliefs which he expressed in many letters to his friends, especially in his early adult years. He was particularly concerned about the influence in the church of the high Anglicans or Puseyites, and he appears to have moved towards a more low church and to some extent an agnostic position in later life.[41] Edward Cowell, a religious man, was always concerned that Khayyám had drawn his friend FitzGerald away from his Christian faith. Writing to Edward Heron-Allen, well after FitzGerald's death, Cowell expressed regret that he had introduced his friend to the Persian poet, whom he viewed as an Epicurean unbeliever.[42]

The agnostic content of the poem contributed both to the initial neglect and subsequent popularity of the *Rubáiyát*, especially because it came to public attention at a time of increasing doubts about and questioning of traditional religious and philosophical values. The first edition was published in the same year (1859) as other seminal books like Charles Darwin's *The Origin of Species* and John Stuart Mill's *On Liberty*. Some religious people, like Edward Cowell, and many readers of *Fraser's Magazine*, would have been disturbed by the poem's questioning of established beliefs. But, for others, Khayyám's thinking, as mediated by Edward FitzGerald, offered an alternative, if less certain, rationale for life to those whose faith had already been shaken. The poem suggests that, while we may not know how or why we came here, or what will happen after our death, we can still take pleasure in today's world of flowers, friends and wine. With the help of these, even '…wilderness is paradise enow' (F1:Q11).

Some readers of FitzGerald's poem have interpreted this acceptance of uncertainty and focus on the joys of the present as being an encouragement to licence and debauchery. The frequent mention of drinking in the verses, e.g. 'Ah! fill the Cup...' (F1:Q37), was taken as referring to the actual consumption of wine and the encouragement of drunkenness; so much so, that, in the early twentieth century, the poem became an object of hatred by teetotal organisations, especially in the USA.[43] In reality, there are only six quatrains in the first edition of the *Rubáiyát* that refer specifically to wine, and most of these relate to the negative effects of drinking, as in 'And much as Wine has play'd the Infidel...' (F1:Q71), or to the ephemeral nature of today's pleasure after which we shall be 'Sans Wine, sans Song, sans Singer, and – sans End' (F1:Q23). As Briggs points out, although the references to drinking (including cup, jug, tavern and grape) are more frequent, nearly 50 in total, there is no sense in the verses of debauchery or using alcohol as a refuge from life, just as there was none in FitzGerald's own life. There has also been extensive debate among experts on how far the references to wine and drinking in Khayyám's verses, and other Persian poetry, should be seen as having a religious significance linked to Súfi imagery. These questions are discussed further by Aminrazavi and Briggs in their recent analyses of Khayyám and FitzGerald's verses.[44]

How the *Rubáiyát* Became Popular

A Total Failure to Start With

As we saw above, FitzGerald had problems with the publication of the *Rubáiyát*. To summarise, after failing to interest *Fraser's Magazine*, FitzGerald himself paid for the printing and gave the little book to Bernard Quaritch the London bookseller for distribution. The unattributed volume was published in late March 1859, and it was a complete failure.

The story of the subsequent discovery of FitzGerald's *Rubáiyát* and its rise to fame is well known.[45] After failing to sell the book, Quaritch put copies into his remainder bin, the so-called 'penny box' since the books were priced at one (old) penny each. Early in 1861, some two years after publication, copies of the *Rubáiyát* were found in this 'penny box' by two literary men, Whitley Stokes and Jack Ormsby. They were excited by the poem, and Stokes showed it to his friends, Dante Gabriel Rossetti and Algernon Swinburne. The latter were also taken by the poem, and went back to buy copies, which the canny bookseller was now pricing at two pence each. The poem became popular among the pre-Raphaelite group and, gradually, it began to be taken up in literary circles.

One early enthusiast was John Ruskin, the well-known connoisseur of art and literature, who, in 1863, wrote a famous letter to 'The Translator of the Rubaiyat of Omar [*sic*]'. At this date, the author of the *Rubáiyát* was still unknown in the UK. Ruskin praised the poem effusively: 'I never did…read anything so glorious', and his letter calls for 'more – more – please more – …'. The letter was given to Edward Burne-Jones, a pre-Raphaelite painter, to be passed on to the anonymous author, when he was identified. Through a chapter of accidents, it took ten years to reach FitzGerald, eventually arriving partly through the good offices of Thomas Carlyle.[46]

Until recently, it was thought that FitzGerald was not recognised as the 'translator' of the *Rubáiyát* until the 1870's. This is true for the general readers of the poem in the UK and USA. But research by John Drew has revealed that, in a footnote to an article on the Persian poem, published in Madras in 1864, Whitley Stokes (one of the people who originally discovered the first edition) mentions FitzGerald's name in this context. The story Drew tells of Whitley Stokes' involvement, two years earlier, with the publication of a pirate edition of the *Rubáiyát* in Madras, and his subsequent publication of his own version of some of the Persian verses, is a fascinating one.[47] FitzGerald himself heard about the pirate edition only in 1872 when he asked Edward Cowell, probably in jest, 'shall I prosecute the Pirate, and try to make some money that way too?' He also commented to Bernard Quaritch, 'So I have lived not in vain, if I have lived to be *Pirated*!' FitzGerald was, in fact, acknowledged as the author of the *Rubáiyát* by Quaritch in a catalogue of rare books issued in autumn 1868, but this was not generally picked up.[48]

Another aspect of the early history of FitzGerald's *Rubáiyát* that has sometimes been neglected is the impact of the initial reviews of the poem in determining attitudes to it. Again, it is only relatively recently that attention has been drawn to a very early review in the *Literary Gazette* of 1st October 1859. This review, while basically positive about the poetry and language of the *Rubáiyát*, condemns it for the fatalism and melancholy of the content, describing it as 'the Gospel of Despair'. Such comments may well have deterred those potential readers who were already worried about the threat to their traditional faith posed by Darwin's theories of human evolution. The next known review of the FitzGerald poem, that of the second edition by an American critic, Charles Norton, published anonymously in the *North American Review* in 1869, is much more unambiguous in its praise: 'There is probably nothing in the mass of English translations or reproductions of the poetry of the East to be compared with this little volume in point of value as *English* poetry.'[49]

The *Rubáiyát* Takes Off in the 1880s

Disputes about the possible impiety and pessimism of the *Rubáiyát of Omar Khayyám* have continued to dog its progress through the century and a half of its existence; they are even still alive today (see page 130). But despite, or perhaps because of, such controversy, from the 1880s onwards FitzGerald's *Rubáiyát* took off in a big way in terms of public interest.[50] In addition to the intrinsic attractiveness of the poem itself, three factors can be seen as contributing to its rise to popularity. These are: big changes in printing technology, which allowed publishers to produce cheaper, higher quality books, and opened the possibility of putting more illustrations in books for the mass market; the development of this mass market in books, thanks to the general rise in affluence and standards of literacy through the nineteenth century; and a growing interest in 'the Orient', including what we now call the Middle East, which reflected the greater number of visitors to the area and the influence of the paintings and drawings they brought back on the imagery used in art and popular culture. The combined effect of these factors rubbed off on FitzGerald's poem, making it a prime candidate for republication.[51]

Much of the initial popular interest in the *Rubáiyát* was created in the USA, thanks especially to the publication of the first illustrated edition by Houghton Mifflin in 1884.[52] This contained the illustrations of Elihu Vedder, an American artist living in Rome, who had long been interested in the *Rubáiyát*. Vedder himself had the idea of producing a special high quality illustrated version of FitzGerald's poem, and he approached a number of US publishers about this. He finally reached agreement with Houghton Mifflin and then spent nearly a year working on the images and the design of the book. The result was an enormous success for the artist, the publisher and the poem. The first edition of the book was sold out within a week, an exhibition of the illustrations drew enormous crowds, and public interest in FitzGerald's work was aroused (Figure 4).

Vedder's work was reproduced in many different editions in subsequent years. Gradually, more versions of the *Rubáiyát* appeared in the UK as well as the USA. Many were legitimate editions, with approval of the copyright holders, but there were also a number of pirated versions, usually of the text only. This publishing of new copies of the *Rubáiyát* was part of a wider interest, almost a craze, for things relating to Omar Khayyám, which developed particularly in the USA at the end of the nineteenth century. It included the formation of Omar Khayyám Clubs by the literary elite in London and Boston.

From the late 1890s, other illustrated editions began to proliferate.[53] At the turn of the century a number of private presses were important in producing high quality limited editions of the *Rubáiyát*, some with black and white wood engravings. But a feature of the first decade of the twentieth century was the exploitation of FitzGerald's poem by commercial publishers for what became known as the 'gift book' market.[54]

These gift books took the form of quality volumes with good bindings, often with colour illustrations, which were intended not just for collectors but for the affluent general customer. Some were large volumes, very similar to what we now call 'coffee table' books, designed to be displayed and admired, rather than to be studied or read in great detail (Figure 5). Others were little books intended to be given as Christmas or birthday gifts to family and friends; some were very small miniature editions, including a Waistcoat Pocket Classics version. As now, there were also gift calendars, with decorations, illustrations and often some verses from a well-known poem. FitzGerald's *Rubáiyát* was an ideal subject for this kind of treatment, and it appeared frequently in the early 1900s in all of these formats. We know of over 250 editions of the poem in new formats that appeared between 1900 and 1914, and there were probably more than this. In 1909 alone, almost 40 new versions of the *Rubáiyát* came on the market, including some reissues of older editions, with which the publisher was aiming to capitalise on the twin anniversaries, of the first publication and FitzGerald's birth, which occurred in that year.[55]

Interest Sustained Through the Twentieth Century

As our chart (Figure 10) shows, the anniversary year of 1909 represented a peak in the publication of FitzGerald's *Rubáiyát*. But it was by no means the end of the *Rubáiyát* story. The inclusion of the *Rubáiyát* among the gift books, together with its extensive illustration, had widened interest in the *Rubáiyát,* and the poem continued to be republished right throughout the twentieth century, and up to the present time. Even through the difficult periods of the two World Wars, new editions of the poem were published on a regular basis.

However, as might be expected, the nature of *Rubáiyát* publishing has changed over the past 100 years, in line with the evolution of book publishing and public taste. Private presses have remained a continual source of new editions, often with fine bindings and illustrations, and intended for the collectors' market. But after the First World War, the commercial publishers largely forsook the tradition of the Edwardian gift book, especially in its large format. For the *Rubáiyát*, the gift

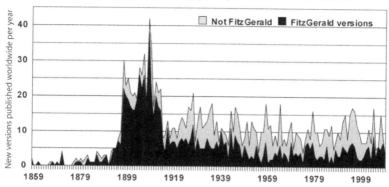

Figure 10 Chart showing all known versions of the *Rubáiyát of Omar Khayyám* published worldwide, 1859–2010.

book was replaced by the special editions produced by new 'heritage' publishers like the Folio Society in the UK and Peter Pauper Press and the Heritage Club in the USA. Commercial publishers have more often produced cheaper, more popular editions, including paperbacks, though there have, from time to time, been some important new illustrated editions from major publishers such as Collins in the UK and Thomas Crowell in the USA.

Worldwide Spread and Influence

The *Rubáiyát* Enters Our Culture

Over the century and half of its existence, readers have reacted to FitzGerald's *Rubáiyát* in many different ways. We have seen how the apparent agnosticism has been a source of controversy, and has, at times, produced fierce debates about the suitability of the poem as general reading. It is clear, also, that the short poem has been a source of solace to people who found themselves in difficult situations. A particular instance is the soldiers fighting in the two World Wars. There are existing copies of the *Rubáiyát* which show, from their annotations, that they were carried by men in their kit bags; the small size of the pocket editions of the poem made it very suitable for this purpose. The dedications on the flyleaves of copies of the poem also provide interesting insights into the role of the verses. The books were frequently given to loved ones, with inscriptions that tell a social history of their own.

During the first half of the last century there were few educated families in the UK who did not possess a copy of FitzGerald's *Rubáiyát*. Many of us have received such copies from our grandparents, and the older generation could often quote great chunks of the poem by heart. In the 1940s and 50s, the *Oxford Dictionary of Quotations* contained over half the lines from the first edition of the *Rubáiyát*, a higher proportion than for any other single work, including the Bible and Shakespeare's works. The number of verses included in the latest, 2009, edition of the *Dictionary* is less than 20, but the poem has become sufficiently well known that certain lines are part of the cultural heritage of the English-speaking world. People like Martin Luther King and Bill Clinton have quoted, in major speeches, from quatrain 51 in the first edition: 'The Moving Finger writes; and having writ / Moves on…' and most people recognise this as a quotation, even if many now have difficulty in saying where the excerpt comes from. Other sayings, such as 'all a chequer-board of nights and days' (F1:Q49) and 'wilderness is paradise enow' (F1:Q11), have become a recognisable part of our language.

FitzGerald's *Rubáiyát* has had more specific literary influences as well. We saw earlier how writers such as Algernon Swinburne and John Ruskin were among those who recognised early on the quality of FitzGerald's poetry. Swinburne called the quatrains '… the sublimation of elegance, the apotheosis of distinction, the transfiguration of grace.' He also borrowed FitzGerald's verse form in one of his later writings.[56] Many other literary figures of the late nineteenth and early twentieth century were influenced by the *Rubáiyát*. We shall see how some of them were provoked to write imitations or parodies of the poem. Other writers, such as T. S. Eliot, acknowledged the influence the *Rubáiyát* had on their own early development. Eliot was greatly attracted by FitzGerald's verse in his teens, though he later rejected this influence on the grounds of the poem's pessimism.[57] Recent research on the position of the *Rubáiyát* within English literature has been summarised in several volumes designed to celebrate the anniversaries of FitzGerald and his Rubaiyat in 2009.[58]

Stimulating International Interest in Omar Khayyám

The great success of FitzGerald's *Rubáiyát* from the late nineteenth century stimulated many people to look again at the mediaeval Persian work that inspired the English poem. More academics and linguists began to study the original Persian text, and to investigate who might be the real author (or authors) of the verses generally attributed to Omar Khayyám.

Results from this research have been outlined in our earlier discussions of the *Rubáiyát* and its two authors. The narrowing down of the number of quatrains actually attributable to Omar Khayyám, the questioning of whether the historical Khayyám – the astronomer and mathematician – was also the author of the verses, the detailed investigation of how FitzGerald interpreted the Persian original; all these stem from research work begun towards the end of the nineteenth century and carried further over the past 100 years. Some of the latest contributions to this work were discussed in a conference on *The Legacy of Omar Khayyám* held in Leiden in 2009.[59] As we have seen, despite all the work that has been carried out, there are still many unanswered questions.

A further consequence of the rise to popularity of FitzGerald's *Rubáiyát* is the stimulus it gave to scholars and writers to create new versions of Omar Khayyám's *Rubáiyát*. From the 1880s onwards, there have been new English translations from the Persian.[60] Some of these were stimulated by the dissatisfaction felt by Persian scholars with the free quality of FitzGerald's interpretation. An early version was that by E. H. Whinfield, who translated some 500 quatrains taken from a number of manuscripts, including the Ouseley and Calcutta texts used by FitzGerald. In 1898, Edward Heron-Allen published his own verse translation of the Ouseley manuscript, before going on a year later to present a fairly literal translation of all the quatrains that he believed FitzGerald had used for each of his verses (examples are given on page 106–7). Some subsequent English versions of the *Rubáiyát* were quite parasitical in nature, taking literal versions such as that by Heron-Allen and converting them into verses that they considered preferable to those of FitzGerald. One such re-interpretation by Richard Le Gallienne, first published in 1897, was for a time very popular.[61] A more recent collaboration, based on original scholarship, was that between the Persian expert Peter Avery and the poet John Heath-Stubbs, published by Allen Lane/Penguin in 1979.

In addition to these new versions in English, over the past century there have been many new editions of the *Rubáiyát* issued in non-English-speaking countries. At the latest count, verses from the *Rubáiyát* can be read in over 85 different languages. Some of these foreign language editions are translations from FitzGerald's English version; others are based on a fresh look at the original Persian text, or sometimes some intermediary version such as a French, German or Russian translation. Among the countries with a particular interest in the *Rubáiyát*, as measured by the number of local versions that have been published, are the Netherlands, Germany, France and the Spanish speaking world. There is also an important involvement in research on and publication of the *Rubáiyát* in Russia, with a subsidiary focus of interest in the central Asian countries, where a version of Persian is one of the local languages. Even in Japan, there is considerable awareness of the *Rubáiyát* of Omar Khayyám. A well-known Japanese version of the poem by R. Ogawa has been reprinted by publisher Otsuko Shinichi over 50 times.

The Iranians Look Again at Their Heritage

One other interesting effect of the popularity of the *Rubáiyát* in the West is the way FitzGerald's work gradually prompted scholars in Iran to look again at Khayyám as a poet. We have noted that the verses attributed to Khayyám have not been considered as among the top flight of Persian literature, although the historical Khayyám has been, and still is, widely revered for his scientific achievements.[62] From the 1920s onwards, Iranian scholars began to investigate more closely both the Persian texts of the *Rubáiyát* and the life of their supposed creator. In 1923 and 1934 a noted Iranian author, Sádeq Hedáyat, published analyses of the text and its authenticity, and this work was followed up by Foroughi and Ghani in 1942. Their combined assessment of the quatrains most likely to be by Khayyám are often taken as being among the most authoritative; their selection of verses overlaps only to some degree, and together they give a total of 235 Persian quatrains, which were used by Peter Avery and John Heath-Stubbs for their 1979 English version of the poem. Another Iranian scholar, Ali Dashti, has since suggested that only 36 'key' quatrains attributed to Khayyám should be accepted as 'authentic', though he also provides a longer list of 75 o-called 'selected' quatrains.[63]

Western interest and the growing amount of individual travel to and ı Iran have helped to stimulate the publication of many new editions *Rubáiyát* in Iran. Since the middle twentieth century, there have ver 40 such versions, often multi-lingual and heavily decorated ıstrated. These appear to be designed both for the tourist and ctors' market, including local Iranians among the latter. After t the time of the Islamic revolution in 1979, the publication multi-lingual versions of the *Rubáiyát* has built up again, since the middle 1990s. Some of the latest editions are in presentation than almost anything seen in recent time in his sense the Iranians seem to have taken up the mantle of 'blishers who produced the *Rubáiyát* as a gift book in the od.

Exploitation in Many Forms

A Stimulus to Creative Activities, and Much More

The popularity of FitzGerald's *Rubáiyát* from the late nineteenth century has been exploited in many different ways. Certain of the derivatives fall into the category of serious creative work, including the drawings and paintings of illustrators and other artists inspired by the poem and musical works of all kinds either setting the words or invoking the atmosphere of the *Rubáiyát*, as well as plays, dances, and more. At the other end of the spectrum, phrases from the poem, and the name and image of Omar Khayyám have been widely used as a basis for branding and product promotion, from the late nineteenth century up to the present day. Somewhere, in between the two, are the large number of parodies of the poem that have been produced over the years, particularly in the early part of the twentieth century. There have also been forgeries of the original Persian text, which have played a significant role in the history of *Rubáiyát* scholarship.

Each main type of *Rubáiyát* derivative is discussed briefly below. This is an aspect of the story of FitzGerald's *Rubáiyát* that has not often been investigated and it deserves more attention.

Rubáiyát Artwork Since 1884

As was mentioned above, the first illustrated edition of the *Rubáiyát*, published by Houghton Mifflin in 1884 with designs and artwork by Elihu Vedder, had an important influence in bringing FitzGerald's poem to a wider audience, and propelling it on the road to great popularity. Vedder's seminal work also led to a fashion for illustrated versions of the *Rubáiyát* which has helped to maintain interest in the poem over the years.

We have documented in detail the extensive range of illustrations created for the *Rubáiyát* over the 125 years since Vedder's publication.[64]

There are few other books, and no individual poems, that have been so much illustrated. FitzGerald's poem has been an inspiration to over 150 different artists, while other versions of the Persian original in many languages have been accompanied by the work of yet more illustrators. Over the whole 150 years since FitzGerald's *Rubáiyát* was first published, almost half the new editions have been illustrated to some degree. The extent varies from one simple frontispiece to several full sets of illustrations for each of the 75 quatrains in the first edition. Our chart above (page 115) shows the trend in illustrated editions of FitzGerald's poem over the whole period. There has been a tendency for more of the foreign language editions to be illustrated in the more recent period, reflecting particularly the emergence of the Iranian publishers with their lavish productions of multi-lingual editions of the *Rubáiyát*.

As might be expected, the nature and style of *Rubáiyát* illustrations have changed over the years, reflecting the evolution of artwork over the twentieth century. The classical and art nouveau styles of earlier artists were followed by more art deco work in the interwar years. Since the Second World War, imagery and presentation have been more eclectic, though there are few very modern or abstract illustrations, even in recent editions of the *Rubáiyát*. There has also been little use of photography as a basis for *Rubáiyát* illustration, despite the enormous role that photographs now play in creating popular imagery. Some publishers have gone back to the tradition of Persian miniatures for their sources, and there are many reissues of the earlier famous illustrations of the Edwardian period, notably those by Edmund Dulac, Gilbert James, René Bull and Edmund Sullivan, as well as the original Vedder work.

An interesting aspect of *Rubáiyát* illustrations is how few of the artists were significantly involved in other kinds of painting and art work. A major exception is Sir Frank Brangwyn, the artistic polymath of the first part of the twentieth century who created two portfolios of paintings for the *Rubáiyát* in 1906 and 1910. Some *Rubáiyát* artists were also fashion and poster designers, like Anne Fish in the 1920s, or cartoonists, like Robert Sherriffs in the middle of the century. But many were painters or engravers who focussed almost entirely on illustration work. Another feature of note is the limited availability today of the original artwork for the illustrations created over many years. Vedder's work is an exception; his original drawings have quite often been on show in the USA, recently in Phoenix, Arizona, as part of the anniversary celebrations of 2009. Certain other libraries and some private collectors hold some artwork that was used, or was intended to be used, to illustrate copies of the *Rubáiyát*. Some work by Cecil B. Trew was on show in an exhibition at the Harry Ransom Center in Austin, Texas in 2009, and the National Art Library holds some originals by Ronald Balfour that were used for a *Rubáiyát* published in 1922. But such examples are relatively few in number, and much original artwork seems to have disappeared from view (Figure 6).

Music, Plays and Dance

Musicians as well as visual artists have found creative stimulus from the *Rubáiyát*.[65] Composers from all genres have set verses from the *Rubáiyát* to music, or found their inspiration from the poem. The first known of these is the classical musician and former singer Liza Lehmann, who in 1896 produced a set of songs called the *Rose Garden of Persia* for soprano, alto, tenor and bass, with piano accompaniment, using 22 quatrains from different editions of FitzGerald's poem (Figure 7). Quite a number of other musicians of the Edwardian period made similar settings of some verses with string and/or piano accompaniment. At the other end of the classical scale, Sir Granville Bantock created an immense three part oratorio for soloists, choir and orchestra, using all the 101 quatrains from the fifth edition; this three hour work was premiered in 1906–09.

Many early compositions based on the *Rubáiyát* have been recorded subsequently and some are available on disk today.[66] More recently other classical composers have set verses for a variety of musical forces, often for unaccompanied choral groups. They include some well-known figures like Paul Hindemith and Krzysztof Penderecki. In 1975, the American Armenian composer Alan Hovhannes created an orchestral suite with a spoken recitation of 12 of FitzGerald's verses (including one repeat).

In addition to different classical settings, various jazz, pop and world music artists have all used the *Rubáiyát* as a basis for their works. Among the better-known jazz creations is a suite by the American composer and performer Dorothy Ashby, with very eclectic instrumentation, while the folk singer Woody Guthrie adapted a number of quatrains in his *Hard Travellin'* series. The famous Egyptian singer Om Kolthom performed and recorded some of the *Rubáiyát* of Omar Khayyám in Arabic translation, while there are recordings of the original Persian text presented as a mixture of recitation and song with traditional musical accompaniment. More recently several disks with Persian and English texts have appeared in the USA and elsewhere, some performed by a mixture of Persian and western artists, with crossover music from both these sources.

Since the early years of the twentieth century, writers have made interpretations from FitzGerald's text in the form of plays, operas and other performing scripts. In some cases, different verses were allocated to specific characters; one such has a poet, his friends, an angel, an innkeeper and others, while Granville Bantock did something similar in his oratorio setting of the whole poem. Dance and pageant settings of the poem were also made, with the idea that these would be accompanied by some of the music inspired by the *Rubáiyát*, for example the Liza Lehmann setting mentioned above. Slightly later came the first of several films about Omar Khayyám and his life; the creation of these was a direct response to the considerable popularity of the *Rubáiyát*, though their story lines have little in common with what is known about the life of the historical Omar Khayyám. A film, *The Life, Loves and Adventures of Omar Khayyám*, produced in Hollywood with Cornel Wilde in the title role, had a musical score by a well-known American composer of film music, Victor Young. The latest film in this tradition, *The Keeper*, with music mainly by Elton Ahi, appeared as recently as 2005.[67]

The Story of the Great Omar

The text of FitzGerald's *Rubáiyát* has been the basis for a variety of creative work. But one copy of FitzGerald's *Rubáiyát* has become sufficiently famous in its own right to create its own mythology. This is the so-called 'Great Omar', an edition produced by the famous bookbinders Sangorski & Sutcliffe.

This finely bound and jewelled volume had a dramatic history. In the early 1900s, the *Rubáiyát* attracted the attention of Francis Sangorski, a partner in the bookbinding firm. Sangorski wanted to create a masterpiece, intended to be the 'greatest modern binding in the world'. He worked for two years on what became the 'Great Omar', finally finishing his fabulous jewelled and inlaid binding of Elihu Vedder's illustrated edition in 1911.

Unfortunately there were problems in agreeing the sale of the book and, in the event, it ended up being shipped to the USA in 1912, when it was lost with the Titanic. Shortly after, Sangorski himself was drowned while bathing. Stanley Bray, who worked for Sangorski & Sutcliffe, produced a re-creation of the original in the 1930s, but this second version was destroyed in the London Blitz in World War Two. Nothing daunted, on his retirement in 1985, Stanley Bray started work on creating the third 'Great Omar'.

This amazing volume has so far avoided any further disasters, and it is now on indefinite loan to the British Library. The work took Stanley Bray four years and was completed in 1989. The binding, modelled on the 1911 original, includes detailed work on the insides of the covers as well as on the front and back. The morocco leather is inlaid and tooled in gold, with a design featuring peacocks and grapes on the upper cover. In total there are some 1000 jewels set into the covers, including topazes, turquoises, amethysts, garnets, olivines and an emerald; many were salvaged from the second 'Great Omar' since the jewels survived the fire in the London Blitz. The original designs were also saved, and the original cover has been digitally re-created as a poster.

The story of the Great Omar has been documented several times, notably in 2001.[68] It is thought that it inspired the novel *Samarkand*, by Amin Maalouf, which features the loss of a *Rubáiyát* manuscript on the Titanic. The novel also recounts the fictional story of Omar Khayyám's supposed friendship with the vizier, Nizám al Mulk, and the assassin, Hasan Sabbáh, mentioned on page 93 above.[69]

Parodies Become Fashionable

The influence of FitzGerald's *Rubáiyát* on later writers has been discussed above. There is, in addition, an important further by-product from the poem in the shape of parodies, which have taken many forms. They range from an adaptation of FitzGerald's lines to apply to other subjects, either comically or seriously, to the simple use of the poetic structure of the four-line quatrain with its unusual AABA rhyming scheme to create what is effectively a new poem.[70] An example from a modern poet, Wendy Cope, based on quatrain 11 from FitzGerald's first edition, illustrates the possibilities:

> Here with a Bag of Crisps beneath the Bough
> A Can of Beer, a Radio – and Thou
> Beside me half-asleep in Brockwell Park
> And Brockwell Park is Paradise enow.[71]

Parodies of the *Rubáiyát* were particularly popular from the 1880s up to the beginning of the First World War. The first known parody was produced by Rudyard Kipling in his *Departmental Ditties* in 1886. Called *'The Rupaiyat of Omar Kal'vin'*, this is an appropriation of the *rubáiyát* form to satirise the financial action of an Indian government official. Later examples of this genre include *Rubáiyát* of Golfers, Smokers, Motorists and many more. Potter's *Bibliography* lists over 200 different parodies published in book or article form up to 1929; many of these have appropriate, sometimes very comical, illustrations.[72]

Some parodies have a more serious intent. There are a few created by the troops in wartime, mainly in the First World War, where the authors philosophise about their own predicament using phrases from FitzGerald's poem. Others from this period complain in *rubáiyát* form about the conditions in which they find themselves; *The Rubáiyát of a Maconochie Ration*, by a certain T. I. N. Opener, sets out the author's reaction to a type of food offered to the British troops in the trenches. Later on, in 1934, Duane Edwin Fox produced a *Depression Rubáiyát* adapting 101 verses mainly from FitzGerald's fourth edition; he interprets the problems of the earlier financial crisis in a manner that has resonance for modern times.[73]

Popularity Brings Forgeries

A more disturbing consequence of the poem's popularity has been the appearance during the twentieth century of forgeries designed to make money out of unsuspecting collectors and enthusiasts. The most important of these forgeries have been those of early Persian manuscripts which purported to be previously unknown versions of Omar Khayyám's *Rubáiyát*. Two particular incidents of such forgery were the source of much concern and some embarrassment to the experts who came into contact with them. In both cases, before the deception was discovered, the fraudulent texts were used as the basis for new translations or interpretations of the *Rubáiyát*.[74]

In order to understand what seems like gullibility on the part of experts, it is important to realise how highly anyone working in the field would value any manuscript that appeared to give a more authoritative version of Khayyám's *Rubáiyát*. The uncertainties about the authenticity of the known Persian texts were outlined above. It is therefore not surprising that, when a thirteenth-century manuscript apparently of the *Rubáiyát* of Omar Khayyám appeared on the book market in 1947, experts were very excited. The manuscript was bought by the Chester Beatty Library in Dublin, and it was authenticated by A. J. Arberry, who was professor of Arabic at Cambridge University, and one of the leading oriental scholars of the day. He made a translation of the verses from the new source, comparing them with other manuscripts, which was published in 1949. When a further new Khayyám manuscript appeared in London in 1950 and was bought by Cambridge University Library, Arberry also published an edition and translation of this version.[75]

Only when a third and then a fourth Khayyám manuscript turned up in the book market did people begin to doubt the authenticity of these documents. After much investigation, it was established that the documents were indeed forgeries, probably fabricated in a workshop in the back streets of Tehran and using as the basis for the text the Fredrich Rosen edition of 1925.[76] Naturally, there were some very red faces in the academic and library worlds. But, it is fair to say, as Scott Jermyn has suggested, that Arberry's work on the new translations was not wasted. The Persian quatrains he used were indeed among the ones that have been attributed to Khayyám, and Arberry's interpretation is of both scholarly and literary interest. Despite this embarrassment, Arberry went on to produce a very valuable work investigating the story and basis of FitzGerald's *Rubáiyát*, published in the anniversary year of 1959.[77]

The second story of *Rubáiyát* forgery and deception came a couple of decades later, and involved a well-known poet, Robert Graves, and two brothers of Afghan origin. One of the latter, called Omar Ali-Shah, brought Graves a literal English translation which he said was based on a twelfth-century manuscript of Khayyám's *Rubáiyát* in Persian, which had only recently been discovered in his Afghan family library. Graves was interested in the challenge of turning the prose verses into what he considered to be good English verse. In the preface to his version of the *Rubáiyát*, published in 1967, Graves is very critical of FitzGerald's work. In due course, however, the Omar Ali-Shah source was proved to be a made up one, the English verses having been taken from Heron-Allen's 1899 work on the sources of FitzGerald's *Rubáiyát*.[78] It is interesting that, despite this exposure, *Rubáiyát* verses attributed to Ali-Shah have since been published in the USA and on the continent, including in translation into German.

Commercial Exploitation of the Omariana Cult

A more acceptable commercial manifestation of the popularity of the *Rubáiyát* has been the way in which the name Omar Khayyám has been used in advertising and promotion from the late nineteenth century onwards. This was a particular feature of the craze for Omariana that developed in the USA after the publication in 1884 of the edition of the *Rubáiyát* illustrated by Elihu Vedder. The craze has been documented in some detail by Michelle Kaiserlian,[79] and there were many examples on display in the anniversary exhibition in the Harry Ransom Center in Texas in 2009. In the period before the Second World War, products promoted using the *Rubáiyát of Omar Khayyám* as a 'brand' included cigarettes, tooth powder and dried milk, as well as tearooms and distilleries. The *Rubáiyát* was also used as a theme for the New Orleans Mardi Gras parade in 1905.

What is interesting about this commercial exploitation is that it is Omar Khayyám himself, the supposed Persian author of the *Rubáiyát*, who is often used to create the 'brand identity'. His is the visual image that is displayed, along with appropriate oriental decoration, even though any accompanying words are usually taken from FitzGerald's English verses. The focus on Khayyám was maintained in subsequent use of the *Rubáiyát* for marketing purposes through the twentieth century, something which has spread from the USA and the UK to other countries, including India and the Middle East. Even today wine from India and Egypt, and services such as hotels and restaurants, use the Omar Khayyám brand (Figure 8).

Most people, who recognise the name of Khayyám as something oriental, would not now associate it immediately with a poem translated by a Victorian Englishman. But, without FitzGerald's work, Omar Khayyám, despite his scientific achievements, would be much less well-known in the world outside his home country.

Relevance to the Modern Day

The *Rubáiyát* is Still Being Published

The *Rubáiyát of Omar Khayyám* is less popular now, than it was in the early twentieth century. But it is probably still one of the best-known individual poems on a worldwide basis. The fact that the *Rubáiyát* has continued to be published into the new millennium suggests that it retains its appeal to a new generation of readers.[80]

On a conservative estimate, the *Rubáiyát* has been published worldwide in nearly 100 new formats since the start of 2000, an average of almost 10 a year. Of these, the great majority (85%) were completely new editions and the remainder (15%) reprints of older versions. Over half the new publications contained verses from FitzGerald's version of the poem in English and, among the countries of publication other than the UK and the USA, Iran and France are prominent. A number of new editions have been offered by on-demand digital publishers. Illustrated versions are still popular, accounting for over one in three of the new versions, though there have been relatively few new commissions of artwork for the *Rubáiyát*. One notable exception is the new edition produced by The Folio Society in the anniversary year of 2009. This large collectors' edition has a special fine binding, and contains 16 colour plates based on new work by an artist of Thai origins, Niroot Puttapipat.[81]

The Anniversary Year of 2009

2009 marked the 150th anniversary of the first publication of FitzGerald's *Rubáiyát*, and the bicentenary of Edward FitzGerald's birth. At least four new editions of FitzGerald's full *Rubáiyát* were published to mark these events. In addition to the large Folio Society edition already mentioned, these included two smaller editions with scholarly commentaries, designed to encourage people to look again at a poem that is an important part of our literary heritage. There were some additional publications of selections of verses in other languages.

Many varied events took place during the anniversary year, all of which brought the *Rubáiyát*, Khayyám and FitzGerald, to wider public attention in different ways.[82] There were major exhibitions held in the UK, USA and the Netherlands, focusing on different aspects of the multi-faceted *Rubáiyát* story. Academic conferences in the Universities of Leiden (in the Netherlands) and Cambridge (UK) brought together scholars from English literature, oriental studies and other disciplines, to examine and evaluate the heritage from the *Rubáiyát* and the state of *Rubáiyát* studies today. Newspaper articles and media programmes helped to widen awareness of the *Rubáiyát* and its influence; of particular interest was an hour-long BBC documentary entitled *The Genius of Omar Khayyám*, which was presented by Sádeq Saba, and shown several times on BBC TV channels in 2009 and 2010.[83] Schools' projects and art competitions were also held during 2008–09, highlighting how the poem can still inspire a range of creative activities in painting, dance, music and more (Figure 9 – a prize-winner in 2009).

Some Modern Comments and Controversies

It is a tribute to the quality of FitzGerald's *Rubáiyát* that controversy and discussion about the poem continue into the present day. Recent publications and the events that took place around the anniversary year of 2009 have thrown up a variety of topical questions. We summarise a few key topics here; interested readers are referred to the relevant publications where the issues are set out in full.[84]

A prevailing theme of the discussions about FitzGerald's *Rubáiyát* over the past couple of years has been whether the poem is basically pessimistic or optimistic; is the view of life presented in the *Rubáiyát* a depressing and negative one, or more cheerful and positive? This theme has been highlighted by the voices of two staunch protagonists of the different views, Daniel Karlin and Anthony Briggs. Their views were given in their new editions of FitzGerald's *Rubáiyát,* which appeared early in 2009, and they have written and discussed their views on subsequent occasions.[85]

Another question which has had some prominence in recent analyses of the *Rubáiyát* is that of the sexual orientation of the poem, and, by inference, that of its English author. As discussed earlier (page 99), FitzGerald's male friendships, particularly those with a number of younger men, have led researchers to suggest that he was probably homosexual in orientation, though there is no direct evidence of this. Recent papers by Dick Davis and Eric Gray have looked at the theme of friendship that runs through the poem and considered the influence that FitzGerald's possible homosexuality may have had on his work on the *Rubáiyát;* Gray has specifically examined the text of the poem for its use of homoerotic imagery.[86]

A final topic brought out by a number of pieces of recent research relating to FitzGerald's *Rubáiyát* is the way in which factors beyond the author's and publisher's control combine to bring a literary work to popular attention. In the case of the *Rubáiyát,* the social and religious climate into which it appeared, the economic conditions and state of the book market and publishing industry, the opening up of the Orient as an area of public interest, and the contributions of other individuals who became *Rubáiyát* enthusiasts, all played a part in the poem's rise to worldwide popularity. Several papers at the FitzGerald Conference in Cambridge in 2009 helped to shed more light on these factors.[87]

A Poem That is Still Relevant

One thing that the experience of the anniversary year of 2009 made very clear was that the poetry and the themes of the *Rubáiyát* still appeal to people of all ages. This is not surprising, for the poem covers universal topics and has an ambivalence of view that is part of its attraction. The ambivalence is brought out in the discussion of the poem's optimism or pessimism; one of the qualities of the *Rubáiyát* is that it can be read in many ways, and even interpreted differently by the same reader at different times.

What virtually all commentators agree about is the quality of FitzGerald's verse and his masterly use of the English language. The combination of the special structure of the Persian *rubái* and FitzGerald's unique turn of phrase is part of what makes the *Rubáiyát* so attractive and memorable. In his 2009 edition of the poem, Briggs has also put up a strong argument for the appreciation of the humour of FitzGerald's writing.[88] Above all, it is the basic focus of the *Rubáiyát* on the human journey from light to dark, and day to night, that gives it continuing relevance. The questions raised by Khayyám and FitzGerald – where do we come from, why are we here, where are we going? – are eternal ones, to which answers will always be sought. The poem does not provide answers to these questions. But Edward FitzGerald's interpretation of an earlier Persian text gives an unmatched description of the situation that we all face:

> Into this Universe, and *why* not knowing,
> Nor *whence*, like Water willy-nilly flowing:
>   And out of it, as Wind along the Waste,
> I know not *whither*, willy-nilly blowing. (F1:Q29)

Notes to Part 2

[1] The story of the *Rubáiyát* and the individuals involved with it is told in detail in Garry Garrard, *A Book of Verse: The Biography of the Rubáiyát of Omar Khayyám* (Stroud: Sutton Publishing, 2007). Historical facts about the life of Omar Khayyám are limited. What is known has been summarised recently in Mehdi Aminrazavi, *The Wine of Wisdom* (Oxford: Oneworld Publications, 2005). Earlier reviews include: B. A. Rosenfeld, 'Umar Khayyám' in *The Encyclopedia of Islam,* new edition, ed. P. J. Bearman et al (Leiden: Brill, 2000), 827–34; John A. Boyle, 'Umar Khayyám: Astronomer, Mathematician and Poet', in *The Cambridge History of Iran,* vol. 4, *The period from the Arab invasion to the Saljuqs,* ed. R. N. Frye (Cambridge: Cambridge University Press, 1975), 658–97.

[2] Hazhir Teimourian, *Omar Khayyám: Poet, Rebel, Astronomer* (Stroud: Sutton Publishing, 2007).

[3] The truth of the story was already being questioned by the late 1890s. See Edward G. Browne, 'Yet More Light on "Umar-i-Khayyám"', in *Royal Asiatic Society* 8 (1899): 409–20.

[4] The situation is summarised in Peter Avery and John Heath-Stubbs, *The Ruba'iyat of Omar Khayyam* (London: Allen Lane, 1979), 18–25. There are more extensive analyses in *The Cambridge History of Iran,* vol. 4, *The period from the Arab invasion to the Saljuqs,* ed. R. N. Frye (Cambridge: Cambridge University Press, 1975).

[5] Aminrazavi, *The Wine of Wisdom,* chap. 6 & 7.

[6] FitzGerald recounted this story in his Introduction to the *Rubáiyát* (see page 74). The original story is told in *Chahár Maqála of Nidhámí-i-'Arúdí-i-Samarqandí* [The Four Discourses of Nizámi Aruzi], trans. Edward G. Browne, reprinted from the *Journal of the Royal Asiatic Society* (July and October 1899) (Cambridge: The Trustees of the 'E. J. W. Gibb Memorial', 1978), 100–01.

[7] See following sources for reviews of the accumulation and subsequent questioning of the quatrains attributable to Khayyám: François de Blois, *Persian Literature: A Bio-Bibliographical Survey,* vol. 5, *Poetry of the Pre-Mongol Period,* 2nd rev. ed. (London: Routledge Curzon, 2004), 299–318; Avery and Heath-Stubbs, *The Ruba'iyat,* 25–31; Swami Govinda Tirtha, *The*

Nectar of Grace: Omar Khayyám's Life and Works (Allahabad: Kitabistan, 1941), xi–xxii, cxxxiii–clxxxii.

[8] See page 120 for comment on the views of some twentieth-century Persian experts.

[9] See notes 1 and 7 above.

[10] Joseph J. Scaliger, *De Emendatione Temporum* (Basel: Lutetiae, 1583); John A. Boyle, 'Omar Khayyám: Astronomer, Mathematician and Poet', *Bulletin of the John Rylands Library* 52, no. 1 (1969): 31–45; K. V. Mardia, 'Omar Khayyám, René Descartes and Solutions to Algebraic Equations', paper presented to Omar Khayyám Club, London, 19 November 1999).

[11] Thomas Hyde, *De Religionis Veterum Persarum* (1700); J. von Hammer, *Geschichte der Schoenen Redekunste Persiens* (Vienna: Heubner und Wolke, 1818); Louisa S. Costello, *The Rose Garden of Persia* (London: Longmans Brown et al., 1845), 66–76. Costello's interpretations of the *Rubáiyát* were earlier published without attribution as 'Specimens of Persian Poetry', in *Fraser's Magazine* 21, no. 124 (1840): 420–23.

[12] For details of FitzGerald's life see e.g. Alfred McKinley Terhune, *The Life of Edward FitzGerald* (New Haven: Yale University Press, 1947), and Robert Bernard Martin, *With Friends Possessed: A Life of Edward FitzGerald* (London: Faber & Faber, 1985).

[13] Letter to Fanny Kemble, 27 February 1872, in Alfred McKinley Terhune and Annabelle Burdick Terhune, eds., *The Letters of Edward FitzGerald,* vol. 3, 4 vols (Princeton: Princeton University Press, 1980), 331.

[14] Terhune, *Life,* 305. Over 1000 of FitzGerald's letters were collected by the Terhunes (see note 13).

[15] Alfred, Lord Tennyson, *Tiresias and other poems* (London: Macmillan and Co., 1885), 1–4, 16–18.

[16] *Letters of Edward FitzGerald to Fanny Kemble, 1871–1883,* ed. W. Aldis Wright (London: Richard Bentley, 1895).

[17] See especially Martin, *With Friends Possessed,* and more recent comments by Davis and Gray (note 86). James Blyth, *Edward FitzGerald & "Posh": "Herring Merchants"* (London: John Long, 1908), provides another perspective on one of FitzGerald's relationships.

[18] One of the most complete collections of all FitzGerald's writings, including many letters, is that by his literary executor W. Aldis Wright: *Letters and Literary Remains of Edward FitzGerald,* 7 vols, ed. W. Aldis Wright (London: Macmillan, 1902–03). A more limited three-volume edition was published in 1889.

[19] George Cowell, *Life and Letters of Edward Byles Cowell* (London: Macmillan, 1904), 8.

[20] Letter to E. B. Cowell, 5 January 1854, in Terhune, *Letters,* vol. 2, 118.

[21] Letter to E. B. Cowell, 3 January 1856, in Terhune, *Letters,* vol. 2, 192.

[22] See e.g. Terhune, *Life,* 203–07; A. J. Arberry, *The Romance of the Rubáiyát* (London: Allen & Unwin, 1959), 13–16.

[23] Letter to George Borrow, 24 May 1857, in Terhune, *Letters,* vol. 2, 277; Letter to E. B. Cowell, 8 December 1857, 305.

[24] Cowell's comments, in a letter to Edward Heron-Allen, are reported in Arberry, *The Romance*, 20; FitzGerald's comments are in a letter to E. B. Cowell, 27 April 1859, in Terhune, *Letters,* vol. 2, 335.

[25] There are more details in the main biographies of FitzGerald, e.g. in Terhune, *Life,* 191–203.

[26] Letter to E. B. Cowell, 5 June 1857, in Terhune, *Letters,* vol. 2, 273.

[27] Terhune, *Life,* 205–07.

[28] The history of FitzGerald's different editions of the *Rubáiyát*, together with a detailed comparison of the texts and changes, is given in Edward FitzGerald, *Rubáiyát of Omar Khayyám: A Critical Edition*, ed. Christopher Decker (Charlottesville: University Press of Virginia, 1997).

[29] Jean Baptiste Nicolas, *Les Quatrains de Khèyam* (Paris: Imprimerie Impériale, 1867).

[30] W. Aldis Wright, ed., *Letters and Literary Remains* (1889) (see note 18).

[31] Terhune, *Life,* 298.

[32] Avery and Heath-Stubbs, *The Ruba'iyat*, 7–10; J. T. P. de Bruijn, *Persian Sufi Poetry* (Richmond: Curzon Press, 1997), 6–13.

[33] Edward FitzGerald, *Rubáiyát of Omar Khayyám,* ed. Dick Davis (Harmondsworth: Penguin Books, 1989), 34–38; Edward FitzGerald, *Rubáiyát of Omar Khayyám,* ed. Daniel Karlin (Oxford: Oxford University Press, 2009), xliii–xlvi; Edward FitzGerald, *Rubáiyát of Omar Khayyám,* ed. Tony Briggs, (London: Orion Books, 2009), xlix–lii.

[34] F1 indicates FitzGerald's first edition; Q2 is quatrain 2 in that edition. Similar abbreviations are used in subsequent quatrain references.

[35] Edward Heron-Allen, *Edward FitzGerald's Rubáiyát of Omar Khayyám* (London: B. Quaritch, 1899); Arberry, *The Romance.*

[36] One of the earliest by J. E. C. [Jessie E. (Mrs H. M.) Cadell], 'The True Omar Khayyám', *Fraser's Magazine* NS 19 (May 1879). This is reproduced in Karlin, *Rubáiyát,* 118–33.

[37] Ali Dashti and L. P. Elwell-Sutton, *In Search of Omar Khayyám* (London: George Allen & Unwin, 1971), 170; Davis, *Rubáiyát*, 3.

[38] Terhune, *Life,* 227.

[39] Daniel Schenker, 'Fugitive Articulation: An Introduction to *The Rubáiyát of Omar Khayyám*', in *Edward FitzGerald's The Rubáiyát of Omar Khayyám,* ed. Harold Bloom (Philadelphia: Chelsea House Publishers, 2004), 66.

[40] Aminrazavi, *The Wine of Wisdom,* chap. 5.

[41] Terhune, *Life,* 57–64.

[42] Cowell's views were initially set out in an unsigned article from which FitzGerald quoted in his own preface: 'Omar Khayyám, the Astronomer-Poet of Persia', in *Calcutta Review* 30, no. 59 (March 1858): 149–62; Cowell's comments to Heron-Allen are quoted in Arberry, *The Romance,* 19–20.

[43] See e.g. Vinni Marie D'Ambrosio, 'Young Eliot's Rebellion', in Bloom, *Edward FitzGerald's The Rubáiyát,* 119–49.

[44] Aminrazavi, *The Wine of Wisdom,* 126–33; Briggs, *Rubáiyát,* xl–xliii.

[45] It has been documented in some detail in Terhune, *Life,* 206–13, and Arberry, *The Romance,* 24–9.

[46] Terhune, *Letters,* vol. 3, 416 and illustration 6.

[47] John Drew, 'The Second (1862 Pirate) Edition of the *Rubáiyát* of Omar Khayyám', in *FitzGerald's Rubáiyát of Omar Khayyám: Popularity and Neglect,* ed. Adrian Poole et al. (London: Anthem Press, 2011).

[48] Letter to E. B. Cowell, 16 January 1862 [72], in Terhune, *Letters,* vol. 3, 320; Letter to Bernard Quaritch, 31 March 1872, 339; Terhune, *Life,* 208.

[49] These reviews are quoted in Karlin, *Rubáiyát,* 95–118, and in Eric Gray, Guest Editor, 'Edward FitzGerald and the *Rubáiyát* of Omar Khayyám', *Victorian Poetry: An Anniversary Issue* 46, no.1 (2008): 105–25.

[50] The large number of new editions of the *Rubáiyát* is documented in Ambrose George Potter, *A Bibliography of the Rubáiyát of Omar Khayyám* (London: Ingpen and Grant, 1929) (reissued Hildesheim: Georg Olms Verlag, 1994).

[51] See William H. Martin and Sandra Mason, 'The Illustration of FitzGerald's *Rubáiyát* and its Contribution to Enduring Popularity', in Poole, *Popularity and Neglect.*

[52] The story of Vedder's *Rubáiyát,* its creation and reception is summarised in Martin and Mason, 'The Illustration of FitzGerald's *Rubáiyát*'.

[53] William H. Martin and Sandra Mason, *The Art of Omar Khayyam: Illustrating FitzGerald's Rubaiyat* (London: I. B. Tauris, 2007).

[54] Michael Felmingham, *The Illustrated Gift Book, 1880–1930* (Aldershot: Wildwood, 1989).

[55] These figures and other data relating to *Rubáiyát* publication are drawn from the editors' own research; initial results from this were given in Martin and Mason, *The Art of Omar Khayyam*.

[56] Schenker, 'Fugitive Articulation', 61.

[57] D'Ambrosio, 'Young Eliot's Rebellion', 140-3.

[58] Poole, *Popularity and Neglect*; Gray, *Victorian Poetry*; Karlin, *Rubáiyát*; Briggs, *Rubáiyát*.

[59] Collected papers from this conference are being prepared for publication.

[60] These are documented in Potter, *A Bibliography*, 101-23.

[61] Adam Talib, 'Le Gallienne's Paraphrase and the Limits of Translation', in Poole, *Popularity and Neglect*.

[62] This was evident from interviews in a recent film for BBC Television (note 83).

[63] See especially Sádeq Hedáyat, *Taráne-há-ye Khayyám* (Tehran: Roschenai, 1934); M. A. Foroughi and Q. Ghani, *Robá'iyát-e Hakím-e Khayyám Níshábúrí* (Tehran: Chap-i Rangin, 1942); Dashti and Elwell-Sutton, *In Search of Omar Khayyám*.

[64] Martin and Mason, *The Art of Omar Khayyam*; William H. Martin and Sandra Mason, 'Khayyam, Omar ix. Illustrations of English Translations of Omar Khayyam's Rubaiyat', http://www.iranica.com/articles/Khayyam-omar-ix-illustrations-of-english-translations (accessed February 2011).

[65] William H. Martin and Sandra Mason, 'Khayyam, Omar x. Musical Works based on the Rubaiyat of Omar Khayyam', http://www.iranica.com/articles/Khayyam-omar-x-musical-works-rubaiyat (accessed February 2011).

[66] Ibid.

[67] Details of the film *The Keeper* are on http://www.greatomar.com/ (accessed February 2011).

[68] Robert J. Shepherd, *Lost on the "Titanic"* (London: Shepherds, Sangorski et al., 2001); J. H. Stonehouse, *The Story of the Great Omar bound by Francis Longius Sangorski and its romantic loss* (London: Fountain Press, 1933). See also Garrard, *A Book of Verse*, 153-7.

[69] Amin Maalouf, *Samarkand*, translated from the French by Russell Harris (London: Quartet Books, 1992).

[70] See Annmarie S. Drury, '"Some for the Glories of the Sole": The *Rubáiyát* and FitzGerald's Sceptical American Parodists', and Parvin Loloi, 'The Vogue of the English *Rubáiyát* and Dedicatory Poems in Honour of Khayyám and FitzGerald', both in Poole, *Popularity and Neglect*.

[71] Extract from Wendy Cope, 'Strugnell's *Rubáiyát*', in *Making Cocoa for Kingsley Amis* (London: Faber, 1986).

[72] Potter, *A Bibliography,* 269–300.

[73] T. I. N. Opener, *The Rubáiyát of a Maconchie Ration* (London: Gay and Hancock, 1919); D. E. Fox, *The Depression Rubáiyát* (New York: Review of Reviews, 1934).

[74] See Elwell-Sutton's Introduction in Dashti and Elwell-Sutton, *In Search of Omar Khayyám,* 18–23; also Garrard, *A Book of Verse,* 100–04, 161–2.

[75] A. J. Arberry, *The Rubá'iyát of Omar Khayyám, edited from a newly discovered manuscript dated 658 (1259–60)* (London: Emery Walker, 1949); A. J. Arberry, *Omar Khayyám, A New Version Based upon Recent Discoveries* (London: J. Murray, 1952).

[76] *The Quatrains of the Learned 'Omar-i-Khayyám', with a Biographical Sketch of Omar and his Poetry*, Introduction and Notes by Frederich Rosen (Berlin: Kaviani Press, 1925).

[77] Scott Jermyn, 'Loaves of Bread and Jugs of Wine: Three Translations of Omar Khayyám' in *Meta: Journal des Traducteur* 34, no. 2 (1989); Arberry, *The Romance.*

[78] Robert Graves and Omar Ali-Shah, *The Rubaiyyat of Omar Khayaam: A new translation with critical commentaries* (London: Cassell, 1967); J. C. E. Bowen, *Translation or Travesty?* (Abingdon: Abbey Press, 1973).

[79] See Michelle Kaiserlian, 'Coping With Modernity: The Omar Cure-All', paper presented at Western Conference On British Studies, Dallas (Fall 2006); Michelle Kaiserlian, 'Omar Sells: American Advertisements based on *The Rubáiyát of Omar Khayyám,* c.1910–1920', in *Early Popular Visual Culture* 6, no. 3 (2008): 257–69.

[80] The figures that follow are from the editors' own research.

[81] *The Rubáiyát of Omar Khayyám, The Astronomer-Poet of Persia,* introduced by A. S. Byatt, illustrated by Niroot Puttapipat (London: The Folio Society, 2009).

[82] A fuller evaluation of the programme and its effect have been published in William H. Martin and Sandra Mason, 'Celebrating the *Rubáiyát* in 2009 – Review and assessment', in *Omariana* 10, no.1 (2010) available online at http://www.omarkhayyamnederland.com (accessed February 2011).

[83] Film *'The Genius of Omar Khayyám'* presented by Sádeq Saba, shown on BBC World and BBC Television (2009–10); background details available at http://www.bbc.co.uk/programmes/b00rs21m (accessed February 2011).

[84] See especially the following: Bloom, *Edward FitzGerald's The Rubáiyát;* Gray, *Victorian Poetry*; Poole, *Popularity and Neglect.*

[85] Briggs, *Rubáiyát;* Karlin, *Rubáiyát.* See also Martin and Mason, 'Celebrating the *Rubáiyát* in 2009'.

[86] Dick Davis, 'Edward FitzGerald, Omar Khayyám and the Tradition of Verse Translations into English', and Eric Gray, 'Common and Queer: Syntax and Sexuality in the *Rubáiyát*', both in Poole, *Popularity and Neglect.*

[87] Martin and Mason, 'The Illustration of FitzGerald's *Rubáiyát*'; see also Michelle Kaiserlian, 'The Imagined Elites of the Omar Khayyám Club', and Garry Garrard, 'Edward Heron-Allen: a Polymath's Approach to FitzGerald's *Rubáiyát of Omar Khayyám*', in Poole, *Popularity and Neglect.*

[88] Briggs, *Rubáiyát,* xl–xlix.

Part 3

Further Notes and References

The Texts Presented – Editors' Notes

Sources of the Text

The original publication details for FitzGerald's first four editions of the Rubaiyat are as follows:

The Rubáiyát of Omar Khayyám, the Astronomer-Poet of Persia, translated into English verse. 1st ed. London: B. Quaritch, 1859. A facsimile edition of this was produced by Quaritch in 2009.

The Rubáiyát of Omar Khayyám, the Astronomer-Poet of Persia, rendered into English verse. 2nd ed. London: B. Quaritch, 1868.

The Rubáiyát of Omar Khayyám, the Astronomer-Poet of Persia, rendered into English verse. 3rd ed. London: B. Quaritch, 1872.

The Rubáiyát of Omar Khayyám, the Astronomer-Poet of Persia, and the Salámán and Absál of Jámi, rendered into English verse. 4th ed. London: B. Quaritch, 1879.

None of these versions were attributed to FitzGerald. The fifth edition, which named FitzGerald as source, was published after his death as:

FitzGerald, Edward. *The Rubáiyát of Omar Khayyám.* 5th ed. In W. Aldis Wright, ed. *Letters and Literary Remains of Edward FitzGerald.* Vol 3. London: Macmillan, 1889.

In presenting the texts of the first, second and fourth editions, we have included the corrections to spellings and points of fact identified by Decker in his recent *Critical Edition* of the *Rubáiyát* texts; (see Further Reading on page 161, for publication details).

As far as possible we have left FitzGerald's texts in the form and style that he chose to present them. One major exception is the numbering system used for the quatrains. FitzGerald used Roman numbers for the quatrains, something that can pose problems for the modern reader (including these editors). So we have taken the decision, both for the poem text and in subsequent references, to replace Roman numerals with the 'western' numbers in common use today. As discussed below, we have also presented composite versions of FitzGerald's Notes and Prefaces combining material from the different editions of the *Rubáiyát*.

Quatrain Order and Content

FitzGerald added and deleted quatrains in creating the successive editions of his *Rubáiyát*. He also revised the wording of some quatrains, in certain cases quite extensively. We have indicated on the text of the first and second editions which quatrains were deleted in subsequent editions, and which ones, in the second edition, were new to that version; # indicates an addition, and Ø a subsequent deletion. In the table on page 148, we show the way in which the quatrain numbers in different editions can be matched, as well as the main sources of the Persian text probably used by FitzGerald for each quatrain.

FitzGerald's Notes and Prefaces

FitzGerald provided explanatory Notes and Prefaces to each of his versions of the *Rubáiyát*. The bulk of these texts remained the same over the four editions produced in FitzGerald's lifetime, though some wording was revised, extra items were added to later editions and other items were removed. The texts of the Notes and Prefaces presented above are composite ones, based largely on the fourth edition which represents FitzGerald's final thoughts on the points he covered.

In compiling our composite version of FitzGerald's Notes, we have renumbered the notes, making them applicable to all three texts of the poem shown here, and we have divided some of the longer originals into separate notes. The location and numbering of the notes in each of the original editions is indicated in the table on page 154.

FitzGerald put his Prefaces before the poem, but we have chosen to place them after the *Rubáiyát*, so that the reader has a chance to look at the poem first, before considering any commentary. FitzGerald revised the Prefaces for the successive editions. We have shown the full introduction to the fourth edition, together with a section from the second and third editions that was left out in the Preface to the fourth edition, though it was reinstated for the fifth edition published after FitzGerald's death. The content of the addition is interesting; it relates to the question of whether Khayyám was a Súfi, and it was the result of FitzGerald's reading of a French prose version of the *Rubáiyát* attributed to Omar Khayyám (translated by J. B. Nicolas and published in 1867 – see reference below); the Nicolas version also stimulated FitzGerald to add further verses in the second edition of his *Rubáiyát*. Two small sections of the Preface, which FitzGerald removed after the first edition, have been left out, as has a long passage of French text that FitzGerald quoted only in the 'Nicolas' section in the second edition.

In both Notes and Prefaces, FitzGerald included quotations in other languages, mainly in French, but also occasionally in Greek and Latin. We have retained the French content, providing a literal translation of the key items. The one significant Greek passage has been omitted, since FitzGerald himself provided a translation of this. Readers who wish to see the original are referred to Decker's *Critical Edition*.

FitzGerald's Style

FitzGerald had a distinctive style of writing and presenting his text, which, even in his time, was rather old fashioned. Some of his spellings are idiosyncratic as is his use of capital initial letters for many nouns. His punctuation is also inconsistent and unusual, especially his frequent use of the long dash '—'. Apart from the acceptance of Decker's corrections of some clear errors in the text, we have aimed to leave FitzGerald's presentation unaltered, so as to give as much as possible of the flavour of his *Rubáiyát* as he intended it. It is notable that, in the Prefaces, where FitzGerald quotes extensively from Edward Cowell's unsigned article about Khayyám and his *Rubáiyát*, he left Cowell's spellings of proper names unaltered, even though they differed from his own usage.

FitzGerald's References

In his Notes and Prefaces, FitzGerald mentions a number of writers and their works, without giving any further details. To him, as a Victorian man of letters, the references were obvious enough, but today the names and works can seem obscure. Brief details of some of the classical and oriental authors are given in the Glossary. We list below the information available to us on some specific references; these are partly drawn from Decker's work.

Binning, Robert B. M. *Journal of Two Years' Travel in Persia, Ceylon, etc.* London: Wm. H. Allen, 1857.

Carlyle, Thomas. *The Life of John Sterling.* London: Chapman and Hall, 1851.

Cook, James. *A Voyage toward the South Pole, and Round the World...* 2 vols. London: W. Strahan and T. Cadell, 1777.

Cowell, Edward B. (unsigned), 'Omar Khayyám, the Astronomer-Poet of Persia', in *Calcutta Review* 30, no. 59 (March 1858): 149–62. *[This is the review article from which FitzGerald quotes so extensively in his Prefaces.]*

D'Herbelot, Barthélemy. *Bibliotheque orientale, ou Dictionaire universel.* Paris: Compagnie des Libraires, 1697.

Gibbon, Edward. *The History of the Decline and Fall of the Roman Empire.* London: Strahan and Cadell, 1776–89. *[many times reprinted]*

Hyde, Thomas. *Historia religionis veterum Persarum, eorumque Magorum.* Oxford: Theatro Sheldoniano, 1700.

Nicolas, J. B. *Les Quatrains de Khèyam.* Paris: Imprimerie Impériale, 1867.

Thorwaldsen, Bertel. *[He was a Danish sculptor who established a museum of his works, which opened in 1848, and where he was buried. FitzGerald had presumably read a report of the sculptor's wishes for his last resting place.]*

Walton, Izaak. *The lives of Dr Donne, Sir Henry Wotton, Mr Richard Hooker, Mr George Herbert.* London: R. Marriott, 1670. *[many times reprinted]*

Quatrain Numbers in the *Rubáiyát*

FitzGerald inserted and removed quatrains in his successive editions of the *Rubáiyát*, moving from 75 verses in the first edition, up to 110 in the second edition, and down to 101 in the third and subsequent editions. The effect of the changes is to alter the quatrain number of what is essentially the same verse in different editions. The table below provides a basis for identifying the same quatrain in successive editions, so that the exact text and wording (which FitzGerald often also changed) can be compared.

In the table, the quatrains are shown in the order of the second and longest edition. Readers interested in a more extensive set of comparisons are referred to Decker's *Critical Edition*, or to the valuable web site created by Richard Brodie, http://www.therubaiyat.com/fitzindex.htm, which allows the comparison between the verses in the order of any of the four main editions (full references are on pages 161–2).

Our table also indicates, in the final column, the main sources from which FitzGerald took his Persian originals for each quatrain. This analysis draws on the studies of FitzGerald's sources made by Edward Heron-Allen (see note 35, on page 135). In that column, the following code is used:

O is the Ouseley Manuscript from the Bodleian Library in Oxford.
C is the Calcutta Manuscript found in that city by Edward Cowell.
N is the French edition of the *Rubáiyát* published by Nicolas in 1867 (see note 29, on page 135).
A is the poem *Mantiq al-Tayr* [*Conference of the Birds*] by Attár (on which FitzGerald also worked).
F is probably an original creation of Edward FitzGerald.

Number Given to Same Quatrain in Different Editions of FitzGerald's *Rubáiyát*			Persian Sources
1st	2nd	3–5th	
1	1	1	C
2	2	2	C
3	3	3	C
4	4	4	O
5	5	5	F
6	6	6	O
7	7	7	C
	8	8	OC
8	9	9	OC
9	10	10	OC
10	11	11	O
11	12	12	O
12	13	13	OC
	14		O
13	15	14	C
15	16	15	O
14	17	16	C
16	18	17	C
17	19	18	C
	20		C
20	21	21	C
21	22	22	C
22	23	23	C
18	24	19	O
19	25	20	C
23	26	24	O
24	27	25	C
	28		O
25	29	26	OC
27	30	27	OC
28	31	28	OC
29	32	29	OC

(Continued)

(Continued)

Number Given to Same Quatrain in Different Editions of FitzGerald's *Rubáiyát*			Persian Sources
1st	2nd	3–5th	
30	33	30	O
31	34	31	C
32	35	32	OC
	36	33	A
33	37	34	A
34	38	35	OC
35	39	36	O
36	40	37	O
	41	38	C
	42	39	O
	43	40	C
	44		C
47	45	42	OC
48	46	43	C
	47	46	N
	48	47	ON
38	49	48	OC
	50	49	OC
	51	50	OC
	52	51	C
	53	52	C
	54	53	C
	55	41	O
39	56	54	O
40	57	55	C
41	58	56	O
	59	57	OC
42	60	58	C
43	61	59	OC
44	62	60	OA
	63	61	OC

(Continued)

(Continued)

Number Given to Same Quatrain in Different Editions of FitzGerald's *Rubáiyát*			Persian Sources
1st	2nd	3–5th	
	64	62	OC
	65		OC
26	66	63	O
	67	64	C
	68	65	C
	69	44	OC
	70	45	C
	71	66	O
	72	67	O
46	73	68	O
49	74	69	O
50	75	70	C
51	76	71	O
	77		F
52	78	72	O
53	79	73	O
	80	74	O
54	81	75	C
55	82	76	C
56	83	77	O
	84	78	C
	85	79	C
	86		C
57	87	80	O
58	88	81	C
59	89	82	OC
	90	83	O
61	91	84	C
62	92	85	O
63	93	86	F
60	94	87	O

(Continued)

Number Given to Same Quatrain in Different Editions of FitzGerald's *Rubáiyát*			Persian Sources
1st	**2nd**	**3–5th**	
64	95	88	C
65	96	89	OC
66	97	90	O
67	98	91	OC
	99		F
68	100	92	C
69	101	93	C
70	102	94	C
71	103	95	O
72	104	96	C
	105	97	C
	106	98	N
	107		N
73	108	99	C
74	109	100	O
75	110	101	O
37			OC
45			F

Note References in the *Rubáiyát*

FitzGerald inserted and removed notes as well as quatrains in his successive editions of the *Rubáiyát*; he also revised some of the note wordings. In presenting the text above, we have compiled a composite version of FitzGerald's notes, based mainly on the notes to the fourth edition, where FitzGerald gave only a quatrain reference for each note. We have renumbered the notes to make them applicable to all three texts of the poem shown here, and divided some of the longer originals into separate notes. There is one note that was shown only in the first edition, and a few notes are applicable only to the second and/or fourth editions; some relate to the quatrains new in the later editions.

The table below provides a basis for identifying how our composite version of FitzGerald's notes relates to the location and numbering of the notes in each of the original editions.

Composite Notes Note No.	Subject in Brief	Equivalent Notes in FitzGerald's Original Editions					
		First Edition		Second Edition		Fourth Edition	
		Note No.	Quatrain	Note No.	Quatrain	Note No.*	Quatrain
1	Stone	1	1				
2	False dawn	2	2	1	2	1	2
3	New Year	3	4	2	4	2	4
4	White hand of Moses	4	4	3	4		4
5	Iram	5	5	4	5	3	5
6	Pehlevi	6	6	5	6	4	6
7	Red rose	7	6	6	6		6
8	Rustum	8	9	7	10	5	10
9	Drum beaten	9	12	8	13	6	13
10	Rose's golden centre	10	13	9	15	7	14
11	Persepolis	11	17	10	19	8	18
12	Bahrám Gúr	11	17	10	19	8	18
13	Coo, coo, coo/ Mr Binning	11	17	11	20	8	18
14	Pasque flower					8	18/19 #
15	1000 years each planet	12	20	12	21	9	21
16	Saturn, Lord of Seventh Heaven	13	31	13	34	10	31
17	Me and Thee	15 Ø	32	14	35	11	32

| Composite Notes | Subject in Brief | Equivalent Notes in FitzGerald's Original Editions | | | | | |
| | | First Edition | | Second Edition | | Fourth Edition | |
Note No.		Note No.	Quatrain	Note No.	Quatrain	Note No.*	Quatrain
18	Attár story					12	37
19	Wine libation			15	42	13	39
20	Azräel			16	46	14	43
21	Caravan	16	38	17	49		
22	Máh to Máhi			18	52	15	51
23	Jest at Khayyám's studies	14 Ø	41	19	58	16	56
24	72 religions	17	43	20	61	17	59
25	Mahmúd's conquest of India	18	44	21	62	18	60
26	Magic-lanthorn	19	46	22	73	19	68
27	O dánad …	20	50	23	75	20	70
28	Parwín and Mushtarí	21	54	24	81	21	75
29	Pot and potter					22	87
30	Ramazán	22	66	25	97	23	90

* Editors' numbering. FitzGerald only gave quatrain references in the notes to the fourth edition.

Ø Some of FitzGerald's notes to the first edition were not in quatrain sequence. Decker suggests that this may be the result of a late alteration to the quatrain order.

FitzGerald included this note in his reference to quatrain 18 in the fourth edition, but he applied it to quatrain 19.

Glossary of Names and Terms

Name or Term	Meaning
Alif	The first letter in the Arabic and Persian alphabets.
Alp Arslan	Nephew of, and successor to, Seljuk ruler Toghrul Beg (qv).
Attár	A prolific Persian poet of the twelfth century CE, whose work *The Bird Parliament* was also 'translated' by FitzGerald.
Azräel	The angel of death in Islam and some other religions.
Bahrám Gúr	An early Persian king, noted for his pleasure seeking, especially hunting. Gúr means both a wild ass and the grave.
Cabul	Persian spelling of Kabul in present day Afghanistan.
Caravanserai	Inn for travellers.
Eclogue	A short poem generally of a pastoral nature.
Epicurus	An influential Greek philosopher of the 3rd century BCE who advocated a life based on the pursuit of happiness.
Ferrásh	A servant whose special job was to pitch and strike the camp.
Firdausi	Tenth/eleventh-century CE Persian poet, famed as the author of the *Sháh-Náma*.
Ghazni	A city, now in Afghanistan, which was the base of the empire of Sultan Mahmúd (qv).
Háfiz	A Persian poet of the fourteenth century CE.
Hátim Tai	An Arab noted for his generosity.

Iram	A fabulous garden, famous in Islamic poetry.
Ismaili	Refers to a religious grouping of Shi'a Muslims.
Jámi	A Persian poet of the fifteenth century CE.
Jamshýd	An early Persian king of the Peshdádian dynasty (qv), who built the city of Persepolis (qv).
Jeláluddín	A thirteenth-century CE Súfi (qv) poet, better known as Rumi.
Kaikhosrú	The third king of the second Persian dynasty.
Kaikobád	The first king of the second Persian dynasty.
Khorasan	Province in the north-east of Persia.
Kúza-Náma	The Book of the Pots.
Lucretius	A Roman poet and philosopher who lived in the first century BCE and was a follower of the Epicurean school.
Mahmúd	Highly cultured Persian king based in Ghazni (qv), who conquered north-west India.
Malik Shah	Son of Seljuk ruler Alp Arslan (qv). He established an observatory at Isfahán.
Mithkals	A unit of weight in Persia c. 5 grams, usually used for gold.
Naishápúr	Earliest known capital of Khorasan (qv). The birthplace and final resting place of Omar Khayyám.
Nizám al Mulk	Vizier (Prime Minister) to the Seljuk rulers, Alp Arslan and Malik Shah (qv).
Nizámi of Samarcand	Twelfth-century CE Persian writer of prose, famous for his essays in the *Chahár Maqála*.
Ouseley, Sir William	Orientalist of the late eighteenth century/early nineteenth century CE who, among other things, acquired the famous manuscript of the *Rubáiyát* of Omar Khayyám, which is now in the Bodleian Library in Oxford.
Parwín and Mushtarí	The constellation of stars known as the Pleiades and the planet Jupiter.

Pehlevi	Principal language of Persia from the third to eighth centuries CE.
Persepolis	City in the south of Persia established by Jamshýd (qv) and said to have been destroyed by Alexander the Great in 330 BCE.
Peshdádian dynasty	The first royal dynasty of Persia.
Ramazán	The Persian word for the Muslim month of fasting, also known as Ramadán.
Rustum	A mythical Persian warrior, famed in the *Sháh-Náma* (Book of the Kings) by Firdausi (qv). Also written as Rustam.
Sabbáh, Ben	Also known as Hasan as-Sabbáh; the founder/leader of an Ismaili (qv) sect, which became known as 'The Assassins'.
Sassanian dynasty	Dynasty established in Persia in the third century CE and ended in the sixth century CE.
Saturn	A god in many ancient mythologies, who was linked to one of the outer planets of the sun.
Seljuk dynasty	Dynasty established in Persia by Seljuk Turks at the beginning of the eleventh century CE. See also Toghrul Beg, Alp Arslan and Malik Shah.
Seventh Gate	According to some Islamic thinking, the deepest gate of hell.
Súfi, súfism	Refers to followers of a mystical expression of the Islamic faith.
Takhallus	Pen name used by Persian poets.
Tamám (shud)	Literally 'the end (it becomes)'.
Tetrastich	A poem or stanza of four lines.
Toghrul Beg	Chief of the Turkik nomads who invaded Persia in the eleventh century CE, and established the Seljuk dynasty (qv).
Transoxiana	The region north-east of the Oxus river.
Zál	The father of Rustum (qv).

Further Reading
and Online Resources

This short bibliography includes mainly recently published works. There are more extensive references to earlier sources in the notes to Part 2.

Recent Editions of the *Rubáiyát*

Edward FitzGerald. *Rubáiyát of Omar Khayyám.* Edited by Dick Davis. Harmondsworth: Penguin Books, 1989.

Edward FitzGerald. *Rubáiyát of Omar Khayyám: A Critical Edition.* Edited by Christopher Decker. Charlottesville: University Press of Virginia, 1997.

Edward FitzGerald. *Rubáiyát of Omar Khayyám.* Edited by Daniel Karlin. Oxford: Oxford University Press, 2009.

Edward FitzGerald. *Rubáiyát of Omar Khayyám.* Edited by Tony Briggs. London: Orion Books, 2009.

Avery, Peter and John Heath-Stubbs. *The Ruba'iyat of Omar Khayyam.* London: Allen Lane, 1979.

Background on the *Rubáiyát*

Potter, Ambrose G. *A Bibliography of the Rubáiyát of Omar Khayyám.* London: Ingpen and Grant, 1929. Re-issued Hildesheim: Georg Olms Verlag, 1994.

Coumans, Jos. *The Rubáiyát of Omar Khayyám: An Updated Bibliography.* Amsterdam: Leiden University Press, 2010.

Garrard, Garry. *A Book of Verse: The Biography of the Rubáiyát of Omar Khayyám.* Stroud: Sutton Publishing, 2007.

Background on Omar Khayyám

Aminrazavi, Mehdi. *The Wine of Wisdom.* Oxford: Oneworld Publications, 2005.

Teimourian, Hazhir. *Omar Khayyám: Poet, Rebel, Astronomer.* Stroud: Sutton Publishing, 2007.

Background on Edward FitzGerald

Martin, Robert B. *With Friends Possessed: a Life of Edward FitzGerald*. London: Faber & Faber, 1985.

Terhune, Alfred McKinley. *The Life of Edward FitzGerald*. New Haven: Yale University Press, 1947.

Terhune, Alfred McKinley and Annabelle Burdick Terhune, eds. *The Letters of Edward FitzGerald*. 4 vols. Princeton: Princeton University Press, 1980.

Contemporary Analyses Relating to the *Rubáiyát*

Bloom, Harold, ed. *Edward FitzGerald's The Rubáiyát of Omar Khayyám*. Philadelphia: Chelsea House Publishers, 2004.

Collected papers from the conference *The Legacy of Omar Khayyám*, held at the University of Leiden, July 2009 (in preparation for publication).

Gray, Eric, guest ed. 'Edward FitzGerald and the *Rubáiyát* of Omar Khayyám'. *Victorian Poetry: An Anniversary Issue* 46, no. 1 (2008).

Martin, William H. and Sandra Mason. *The Art of Omar Khayyam: Illustrating FitzGerald's Rubaiyat*. London: I. B. Tauris, 2007.

Poole, Adrian et al., eds. *FitzGerald's Rubáiyát of Omar Khayyám: Popularity and Neglect*. London: Anthem Press, 2011.

Online Resources

Brodie, Richard, ed. 'The Rubaiyat of Omar Khayyam: a complete on-line resource'. http://www.therubaiyat.com/index.htm.

Various articles in Encyclopaedia Iranica online, http://www.iranica.com, including the following:

Biegstraaten, Jos. 'Khayyam, Omar xi. Impact on the Literary and Social Scene Abroad'. http://www.iranica.com/articles/khayyam-xi.

Martin, William H. and Sandra Mason. 'Khayyam, Omar ix. Illustrations of English Translations of Omar Khayyam's Rubaiyat'. http://www.iranica.com/articles/khayyam-omar-ix-illustrations-of-english-translations.

Martin, William H. and Sandra Mason. 'Khayyam, Omar x. Musical Works based on the Rubaiyat of Omar Khayyam'. http://www.iranica.com/articles/khayyam-omar-x-musical-works-rubaiyat.

Editors' website on *The Rubaiyat of Omar Khayyam*. http://www.omarkhayyamrubaiyat.com.

Website of the Netherlands Omar Khayyam Society (English language content). http://www.omarkhayyamnederland.com/index.html.

Index

This index includes people and place references in the *Rubáiyát*, as well as specific and subject references in FitzGerald's comments and elsewhere in the book. Where people or organisations have had a special role in relation to the *Rubáiyát of Omar Khayyám* as editor, illustrator, musician, publisher, or translator, this has been indicated after the name.